AF408019

JEZEBEL TO JESUS

*A Memoir of a Broken Girl in
Desperate Need of a Savior*

Nikki Lewis

Copyright © 2024 by Nikki Lewis All right reserved

Cover design by Katarina on fiverr

Scripture quotations are taken from Courage For Life Study Bible for Woman (NLT) by Anne White

Copyright© 1996, 2004, 2012, 2015, 2022, 2023 by Tyndale House Ministries

This is a work of creative non-fiction. All of the events in this memoir are true to the best of the author's memory. Some names and identifying features have been changed to protect the identity of certain parties. The author in no way represents any company, corporation, or brand, mentioned herein. The views expressed in this memoir are solely those of the author.

Acknowledgments

This book is dedicated to my beautiful mother, Lorean Lewis. Your unwavering love has helped shape my understanding of what it truly means to love. The compassion and strength you showed my brother, and I continue to inspire me daily. I miss you every day and will always love you deeply.

CONTENTS

PROLOGUE

Tall, dark, handsome, and successful—these are qualities many women desire in a man. So, when a guy with all these attributes noticed me as I served his drinks, I was astonished. His captivating smile, strong features, and the fact that he was a lawyer instantly drew me in. His presence exuded confidence and sophistication, making it hard to look away. I was mesmerized and had no reservations about succumbing to his charm. When he asked me out, I said yes without hesitation, feeling a flutter of excitement and anticipation.

At 25, fresh out of a toxic relationship, I was yearning for a fresh start. My previous relationship had left me emotionally drained and deeply hurt, with my self-esteem in tatters. The prospect of meeting someone new and exciting seemed like a beacon of hope. Each time he visited the bar, he greeted me with a warm smile and kind demeanor, gradually lifting my spirits. He would engage me in light-hearted conversations, often making me laugh and feel appreciated. His attention felt like a soothing balm on my wounded heart.

I soon found myself eagerly anticipating his visits, counting the hours until I saw him again. His consistent presence became a bright spot in my day, a chance to escape from the shadows of my past. With each encounter, my hope for a new beginning grew stronger. His attention made me feel seen and valued, something I desperately needed after the emotional toll of my previous relationship.

We talked on the phone for several weeks before our first date, and each call made my heart race with excitement. Our conversations were mostly light and casual, but his voice was comforting. I was amazed that someone as handsome, successful, and charming as him could be genuinely interested in me. I savored every moment we talked, often replaying our conversations long after we hung up.

Our phone calls became the highlight of my day. I found myself smiling at my phone, eagerly waiting for his name to appear on the screen. The anticipation of hearing his voice and the thrill of our connection made me feel alive in a way I hadn't felt in a long time.

Each call deepened my infatuation. I imagined our first date and pictured us together, laughing and enjoying each other's company. My mind wandered to the possibilities of what could come next, and I allowed myself to dream of a future where I could finally move on from my past hurts. I felt a renewed sense of hope and optimism, believing that this charming, successful man could be the one to help me rediscover joy and love.

However, as time went on, I started to feel uneasy. Despite our frequent conversations, he was reluctant to share much about himself. His evasiveness began to raise red flags, but I chose to ignore my intuition. His attractiveness and success captivated me, convincing me that these qualities outweighed my growing concerns. My excitement distracted me from the warning signs, and I continued to pursue the relationship, hoping that my unease was just a product of my imagination. I rationalized his distance as a sign of mystery rather than a cause for concern, telling myself that perhaps he was simply a private person.

A nagging sense of doubt tempered my excitement as our date approached. I tried to push it aside, focusing instead on the positive aspects of our connection. When the day finally arrived, I was nervous and eager to see him. I hoped that spending time together in person would dispel the doubts creeping into my mind.

Despite my reservations, I clung to the hope that this new relationship would be different and that it would be the fresh start I so desperately needed.

On our first date, we went to Fridays. He picked me up because I didn't have a car. He was on time and seemed genuinely excited to see me, which momentarily made me forget about my uneasiness. I had carefully chosen my outfit—a black flowy skirt and a red satin button-up top—hoping to make a good impression. He looked sharp in a button-up shirt and slacks, adding to his already striking appearance.

As we settled into our seats at the restaurant, the conversation began to flow, but something felt off. He was still reluctant to answer the standard "date questions"—simple inquiries about his background, interests, and family. His indirectness struck me as odd, and the uneasiness I had felt before the date started to creep back in. Trying to shake off my doubts, I decided to have a drink, hoping it would help me relax.

We stayed at the restaurant for a few hours, but the conversation felt increasingly forced as time passed. I struggled to keep the dialogue going, sensing he was holding back. Despite his charm and good looks, the evening left me feeling more unsettled than before. A growing sense of discomfort overshadowed the initial excitement I had felt.

After the date, he proceeded to take me home, at least I thought, but he drove me to a park instead. It was around 11 p.m., so I instantly became concerned. After parking, we exited his SUV and walked over to a bench. He tried to lay me on the bench to kiss me, but I told him no. He appeared frustrated, which scared me. We then walked back to his car, and he pulled out his penis and started to masturbate. While doing it, he demanded I kiss his neck. I felt too helpless and afraid to say no. After masturbating, he stepped out of the car, came to my side, and began to rape me. He stopped when I started to cry and told me that he didn't want me to think that I had been raped. He finally took me home and dropped me off like nothing had happened.

I cried that entire night. I didn't go to the police, and I didn't tell my family because I couldn't process what had happened. I kept going back and forth on whether he had raped me or not. The lines between consent and coercion were blurred in my mind, leaving me feeling confused and conflicted. I felt embarrassed, angry with myself, and humiliated. God had sent warning signs, but I did not listen, and now I was left to deal with the aftermath.

The sad reality is that I continued talking to him for a while because I felt guilty for not giving him what he wanted. The aftermath of our encounter left me in a state of confusion and self-blame. I questioned my actions and choices, wondering if I had somehow been at fault. I scrutinized every detail of our interactions, searching for something that might explain why things had gone so horribly wrong. Despite the pain he caused me, I couldn't immediately sever our connection. I was trapped in a cycle of guilt and fear, hoping that maintaining some form of communication might lead to understanding or closure.

Each time he called, a part of me hoped for an apology or an explanation that would make sense of the chaos in my mind. I told myself that I could find some semblance of peace if we talked things through. But instead of clarity, each conversation only deepened my confusion and self-doubt. His words were often dismissive and manipulative, making me feel like I was overreacting or imagining things.

I felt trapped in a web of conflicting emotions. On one hand, I wanted to confront him and demand answers. On the other hand, I feared the repercussions of such a confrontation. What if he denied everything? What if he turned the blame on me? These thoughts paralyzed me, leaving me unable to take decisive action.

Despite the trauma, I couldn't help but cling to the remnants of the person I had thought he was. I had invested so much hope and emotion into our relationship that admitting the truth felt like an insurmountable defeat. The idea of being wrong about him, of having misjudged his character so completely, was a blow to my already fragile self-esteem.

My nights were plagued by restless sleep and nightmares. I repeatedly replayed the events, questioning what I could have done differently. My days were a blur of emotional turmoil as I struggled to maintain a facade of normalcy. I became withdrawn and distant.

The cycle of guilt and fear seemed endless. I wanted to believe there was some way to make sense of it all and heal. But the more I tried to rationalize his actions, the more I felt lost and broken. Maintaining contact with him only prolonged my suffering, but I couldn't bring myself to cut him off entirely. It was as if I needed his acknowledgment of what had happened to validate my pain and make it real.

Eventually, I realized that no amount of communication with him would bring the closure I sought. His inability to take responsibility and my struggle with self-forgiveness created a toxic loop that only deepened my wounds. I needed to find a way to heal without him, to reclaim my sense of self-worth.

After I finally mustered the courage to end our communication, he continued to visit the bar where I worked. Initially, he came alone, and I would discreetly ask my co-workers to serve him, avoiding direct contact. Each time he walked in, my heart would race, and a wave of anxiety would wash over me. It was a constant reminder of the trauma, making it hard for me to move on.

But then, he started showing up with another woman. Seeing him with her was like a dagger to my heart. I couldn't understand why he would do that, especially in a place where he knew I worked. It felt deliberate as if he was trying to assert his control or provoke a reaction from me. The sight of them together hurt me deeply, intensifying my feelings of unworthiness and rejection.

I struggled with a whirlwind of emotions, from anger and betrayal to self-doubt and sadness. I couldn't shake the thought that he might treat her better than he treated me, and I often wondered if I deserved this treatment. The idea that I was replaceable and unworthy of genuine affection haunted me. I compared my value to hers unaware that his actions did not reflect my worth.

These thoughts consumed me, eroding my self-esteem and making it difficult to trust again. I felt a deep sense of betrayal and confusion, grappling with the emotional scars left by both my previous toxic relationship and this traumatic experience. My heart hardened, and I became wary of men, fearing that I would only encounter more pain and disappointment.

Despite this, I still longed for the love and connection a healthy relationship could bring. I knew I deserved better, but the journey to believing it and finding the courage to seek it out was fraught with challenges. The experience left me with a complex mix of emotions as I navigated the difficult path of healing and rebuilding my trust in others and myself.

CHAPTER 1

A CHILDHOOD OF LOVE AND ABSENCE

I grew up in the charming town of Deveraux, Georgia, where my childhood was beautiful, all thanks to my mom. As a single parent, she made countless sacrifices for my brother and me, and we adored her for it.

My mom was my superhero. Despite her countless responsibilities and commitments, she always made time for us. I'll forever cherish the memories of her lovingly prepared, delicious home-cooked meals, each a testament to her dedication and love.

Our childhood was a thrilling adventure, thanks to her endless creativity and knack for keeping us engaged. She orchestrated picnics and art projects, ensuring we always had something fun to do. Her enthusiasm and energy were infectious, making every moment with her something to anticipate eagerly.

We took long walks down a country road every week, finding unique rocks that captured our attention. We named them and created imaginative stories around them. I distinctly remember naming one "Holly Rock" after watching Krush Groove with my brother over 50 times. My mother always accompanied us, patiently listening to our creative tales and contributing her insights and ideas.

She actively participated in various school activities, from field trips and PTA meetings to Field Day. Her presence and involvement profoundly impacted me and others, serving as a true source of inspiration.

During elementary school, I faced several physical challenges, including keloids in both ears, being pigeon-toed, and having a lisp. My doctor prescribed shoes with a metal bar in the middle to correct my pigeon-toed condition. Unfortunately, these issues made me a target for relentless bullying. As a sensitive child, the teasing hurt deeply, and I often came home in tears. My mother, however, was always there with a comforting hug, and her unwavering support meant everything to me.

Reflecting on my childhood, I can't help but notice the stark contrast between my mother's presence and my father's absence. Although my mother was always there for us, my father rarely showed up. When he did come around, he tried to be strict with us but never showed any love or affection. It felt like he was going through the motions, attempting to fulfill some obligation without investing time or effort into our lives.

I always yearned for my father's love and attention, hoping to be Daddy's little girl. However, his absence made it clear that he didn't want that role in my life. It was hard to understand why he didn't want to spend time with us or care about our interests and well-being. The pain of his absence lingered, leaving a void in my heart that only a father's love could fill.

I can't forget the many times my father said he was on his way to take us somewhere, only never to show up. As a kid, I eagerly counted down the days until our planned outing, only to be disappointed time and time again. It was hard to understand why he would make promises he couldn't keep, and I always felt let down. Despite this, I still hoped that he would follow through one day and that we would make some great memories together.

On the rare occasions, my father kept his promises, he took my brother and me fishing, an activity we always enjoyed. One day, he told my mom to get us ready because he was taking us fishing. Although anxious about whether he would show up, I was excited, and my heart danced when he finally arrived. However, the excitement was short-lived. Before we could even cast a line, my dad said we needed to stop by his mother's house, a place we barely knew. He left my brother and me there, promising to be back soon.

Hours passed, and we were stranded at a stranger's house, feeling confused and abandoned. It wasn't until that night, just in time to take us home, that he finally showed up.

My father's absence was just one part of the problem. We also had two half-siblings around the same age who were born to a different mother. They would come over to play at our house, but we were never allowed to go to theirs. My mother was very protective of us and did not trust the other woman. As a child, I found it challenging to understand the emotional turmoil my mother experienced when she had to share the love of her life with another woman. It was a confusing and distressing time for me as I tried to navigate through the complexities of adult relationships and emotions.

One day, while we were all at home, the police arrived to arrest our dad. Watching them take him away in handcuffs devastated me. He spent a year in jail, and during that time, we learned to live without him. We no longer had to endure his empty promises and harsh discipline. After his release, he began to visit again, but my mom saw the disappointment on our faces each time, so she ended the relationship. Though he was always welcome to be a part of our lives after that, he never made an effort to do so.

After my mom ended the relationship, she remained single for a while, and life became much more stable for us. She worked at a general store throughout our childhood, a job we loved because she often took us with her. We would play with the store owner's children, creating countless happy memories. One day, in a surprising turn of events, the owners decided that my mom should own the store. Their decision was a testament to her dedication and hard work, and it marked the beginning of a new chapter for our family.

The store had an apartment in the back, a significant upgrade from our previous living situation. Our joy was palpable but soon overshadowed when my mom met a man who moved in with us. Initially, I was hopeful, thinking he might fill the void left by our absent father. However, my excitement quickly turned into dismay as it became clear he wouldn't bring the stability and warmth I had envisioned.

My mother struggled to make ends meet, but everything changed when we moved to the store. She threw a party I will never forget on one of my birthdays. I was turning eight and was beyond excited to show off our new, fancy home and celebrate with my friends. It was a joyful occasion that marked a turning point in our lives.

The party was amazing, and I received everything I had hoped for. My most cherished gift was a tape recorder, which held a special place in my heart. My brother and I spent hours singing and creating rap songs using an improvised microphone. Our favorite activity was performing for our teddy bears and our mother, who always enjoyed our shows.

Despite our enthusiasm, we often worried that our "masterpieces" would be lost in time, and we longed for a way to capture them forever. The tape recorder was the perfect tool to help us do just that. It allowed us to memorialize our music and share it. This gift brought me immense joy and satisfaction; I couldn't wait to use it.

But after the party ended and my friends went home, I noticed something was wrong. My beloved tape recorder and some of the birthday money I'd received were missing. I searched high and low, but they were nowhere to be found.

Feeling frustrated and upset, I went to my mom and told her what had happened. She took swift action and immediately kicked her boyfriend out of our house. At the time, I didn't understand why he was being forced to leave. I begged my mom to let him stay, as I desperately wanted a father figure.

She reluctantly let him stay because she saw the pain I was experiencing. He stayed with us for some time, but eventually, my mom kicked him out again. Each time she did, I would go outside and cry while he waited for his ride, and then I would plead with my mom to let him stay. This continued for months until my mom reached a breaking point.

She finally explained that he had stolen gas, beer from the general store, and my birthday money and tape recorder. I was almost nine and didn't know how to process it. I wanted a father so badly that I was willing to endure mistreatment to have one in my life.

His actions put us in a dire financial situation, ultimately causing my mom to lose the store. This loss also meant losing our home, forcing us to stay with friends. In 1996, we moved to Maryland to be closer to family.

Georgia had been my home for twelve years. It was where we had built our lives and made countless cherished memories. The thought of leaving our friends and school filled my brother and me with sadness and anxiety. Saying goodbye to the familiar surroundings we had grown so fond of was incredibly difficult. The entire experience was overwhelming, as we were uprooted from the only place we had ever known.

Upon arriving in Maryland, I was struck by how different it was from Georgia. The towering buildings and the sheer number of vehicles on the road created a sense of excitement mixed with a tinge of fear. It felt like I had been transported to a whole new world that was fast-paced and bustling with activity. The sheer scale of everything around me was overwhelming. With its constant motion and energy, the urban landscape starkly contrasted our small Georgia town's quiet, familiar surroundings.

Despite feeling intimidated, I was eager to explore and discover Maryland's unique sights and experiences. The bustling streets, diverse neighborhoods, and vibrant cultural scenes were a lot to take in, but they also presented new opportunities for growth and adventure. The transition was challenging, yet it sparked a sense of curiosity and anticipation within me. I looked forward to adapting to this new environment and finding my place in it, even though it meant leaving behind the comfort of the home I had known for so long.

CHAPTER 2
FIRST LOVES AND EARLY LESSONS

When I first moved to Maryland, one of the earliest people I met was my first crush. We often played outside together, and as a 12-year-old, I had no idea how to act around someone I liked. Whenever I caught a glimpse of him, my heart would skip a beat, and I'd feel a rush of excitement coursing through my veins. We spent countless hours playing outside with each other and our friends, our laughter echoing through the neighborhood.

One sunny afternoon, we both decided to get into a relationship. I was nervous and excited since I had never been in a relationship. The thought of being someone's girlfriend was thrilling, but my shyness made things awkward. The prospect of holding hands or even talking about our feelings seemed daunting.

The following day, after agreeing to be in a relationship, I woke up feeling uneasy and unwell. I needed to figure out how to navigate this new territory. My mind was clouded with a million thoughts as I sat through school that day. I kept wondering if he genuinely liked me, if I was good enough for him, and whether I was even old enough to be in a relationship. My shyness only added to my fears, and I was terrified of what people would think of me if they learned about my new status.

These worries consumed me throughout the day, and I found it challenging to concentrate on anything else. The usually interesting lessons felt like a blur, and I barely managed to keep up with my schoolwork. When the school day ended, I got on the bus to go home. That's when I realized that people already knew about our relationship. The realization made me incredibly embarrassed and uncomfortable. My peers' whispers and knowing glances felt like a spotlight shining on my insecurities. I didn't know how to handle the sudden attention, so I hastily broke up with him in a moment of panic. Thus, my first relationship ended after only 24 hours, leaving me relieved and a little heartbroken.

When I was 16, I entered my second relationship after a four-year gap. I believed I was more mature and ready to handle a romantic relationship then. The person I fell for was the same guy I met when I first moved to Maryland. We had played together outside for years before I realized that my feelings for him had deepened beyond friendship.

We dated for about a year, and it was a wonderful relationship. My mom adored him and considered him a son, appreciating his respectful and kind nature. One of my fondest memories is of a thoughtful gift he gave me. I was an enormous fan of NSYNC and would sing along to their songs until my throat hurt. When I learned they were releasing a new album, I was ecstatic and eagerly anticipated its release.

One day, while we were hanging out, he told me he had a surprise. He asked me to close my eyes, and when I opened them, he held the newest NSYNC album. I was elated, as I had never experienced such thoughtful treatment from a male before. It was a moment of pure happiness, and I felt incredibly special and cherished.

Despite the goodness of our relationship, I eventually realized that I wasn't mentally prepared to handle the positive treatment he gave me. Growing up, I had no positive male role models to look up to. The behaviors and actions of my father figures were inconsistent and often disappointing, which led me to assume that all men were like them. This misguided belief caused me to have unrealistic expectations, and as a result, I ended up in unhealthy relationships.

The weight of my unresolved issues and skewed perceptions became too much to bear. I remember breaking up with my second boyfriend at the playground, a place filled with so many happy memories. The decision was hasty and emotionally driven, and I quickly moved on to someone else without taking the time to process my emotions.

At 17, I had already experienced three romantic relationships that ended. Despite the disappointment, I still longed for companionship. During one of my visits to the mall, a place I frequented to escape my thoughts, I met my next boyfriend. While window shopping, he approached me with a confident smile and asked for my number.

He was incredibly charming, and his warm, welcoming smile could light up an entire room. Being around him was always a pleasure; he had a way of making me feel at ease. Our usual meeting spot was in his neighborhood, and even though I had to check with my mom before hanging out with him, we met several times.

At the time, I was still a virgin, while my boyfriend was not. I vividly remember a conversation with a friend at school about losing our virginity. She was deeply in love with her boyfriend and felt ready to take that significant step in their relationship. Inspired by her confidence and believing it was a natural progression, I decided it was time for me to experience that same level of intimacy.

I shared with my boyfriend that I was ready to take our relationship to the next level, and we were both excited about it. After eight months together, it felt like the right time. I remember taking the bus to his house, feeling a mix of anticipation and nervousness. Being more experienced, he guided me through what to expect and gave me instructions.

Afterward, I took the bus back home, my mind swirling with a multitude of emotions. I felt a newfound sense of maturity, but an unexpected emptiness and awkwardness came alongside. My innocence was gone, and with it, a part of my youth that I could never reclaim. The bus ride home was a quiet, reflective journey, marked by the realization that I had crossed a significant threshold in my life.

After the experience, I noticed a shift in my behavior toward him. I became more emotionally attached to him than I had ever been with anyone else, and my desire to spend time with him increased significantly. However, I began to sense a growing distance from him. He often declined whenever I asked him to hang out, citing prior commitments or other plans. This behavior left me confused and uncertain about the future of our relationship.

I recall one instance when I was spending time with my friends, and suddenly, I felt an intense longing for my boyfriend. I decided to call him, but he didn't pick up, and his phone went directly to voicemail. Worry and anxiety set in, and I began calling him repeatedly, but still, there was no response. I started imagining the worst—that something terrible might have happened to him or that he was intentionally avoiding me.

After several calls, he finally answered, but instead of feeling relieved, I was taken aback by his response. He began cursing at me and abruptly told me that our relationship was over. I was stunned and heartbroken. Later, I learned from a mutual friend that he had ended our relationship because he was already involved with someone else.

I was completely shattered when I received this information. I had given him my heart and body and believed we would have a future together. It was a deep emotional blow that left me feeling bewildered. But I was still desperate for love and couldn't bear being alone, so I quickly entered another relationship.

I entered a new romantic relationship at 18 during my senior year of high school. I met him around the same time as my previous boyfriend, and we started as friends. However, it wasn't until after my breakup with my last boyfriend that our friendship blossomed into a romance.

As our relationship developed, my mother had the chance to meet him, and she quickly grew to like him. She appreciated his respectful demeanor. This approval meant a lot and added a layer of reassurance to our relationship.

We spent over a year together, but as time passed, we grew apart. I don't recall the exact reasons for ending the relationship, but I remember parting ways on good terms, grateful for the time we shared.

CHAPTER 3

DANCING THROUGH CHAOS: MY WILD PHASE IN MY EARLY TWENTIES

During my late teens and early twenties, I went through a bit of a wild phase. At 19, I started working part-time as a server in a restaurant, where I was first introduced to alcohol. I vividly remember my very first drink: an Irish car bomb. I ended up having three of them, which left me quite intoxicated. The only clear memory I have from that night is making out with a guy; the rest is a complete blur.

While working at the restaurant, I formed close relationships with the other servers and bartenders. Many were avid clubgoers and knew all the best spots in town. Despite being under the legal drinking age, I gained entry into these venues thanks to their popularity and connections.

One night, I had the opportunity to visit a reggae club—my first nightclub experience. The atmosphere was electrifying, with loud music and people dancing everywhere. The club was packed, and the energy was contagious. As I watched from the sidelines, I couldn't help but notice the women dancing, swaying their hips, and having a great time. We would often pre-game before entering the club, so under the influence of alcohol, I decided to join the crowd and started dancing. I tried to imitate the other women, copying their moves and trying to keep up with the beat.

As the night ended, one of my friends approached me and bluntly told me I didn't know how to dance. I felt stunned and embarrassed by that comment. I genuinely thought I was doing everything the other women were doing and was unaware of my lack of rhythm. It was a humbling experience, and I realized I needed to improve my dance skills to fit in.

Determined to master dancing, I made it my mission to learn. I spent hours in front of my mirror, immersing myself in reggae music and carefully studying my movements. I also closely watched the men and women in the club, analyzing their techniques. From how I moved my hips to the intricate steps of different reggae dances, no detail was too small to overlook. My ultimate goal was to impress both men and women with my dancing skills, leaving them in awe of my talent.

Learning how to dance gave me a newfound sense of confidence, which made me feel more sexy and seductive. As I continued to practice and improve my dance skills, I noticed that I was receiving more attention from men, further bolstering my self-esteem. I developed a new mindset, believing I could attract any man I wanted.

At 20, I was in a new relationship that began unexpectedly during my daily bus commute. One day, I noticed a guy who immediately caught my eye. He was undeniably handsome, with long, curly black hair that cascaded down his shoulders, perfectly framing his face and accentuating his rich caramel complexion. His Dominican and half-black heritage added an intriguing layer to his persona.

Our conversations flowed effortlessly from the start, and it wasn't long before we were dating. The early days of our relationship were filled with joy and excitement. We spent much time together, laughing, exploring new places, and enjoying each other's company. Everything seemed perfect, and I genuinely enjoyed being with him.

However, as the months passed, unease began to creep in. After about three months, I found myself questioning my commitment. At 20, my life revolved around partying with friends and savoring every ounce of freedom. The thought of being tied down in a relationship felt like a potential loss of the vibrant, carefree life I cherished. I wasn't ready to embrace trading my independence for a relationship.

The moment I decided to end the relationship is still etched in my memory. My brother and I were living together in an apartment, and it was during one of his visits that I made my decision. My thoughts were consumed with my desires and the unwavering belief that my happiness should come first. At that point, partying and experiencing life to the fullest were my top priorities.

I felt no sadness or regret when I finally broke up with him. Instead, a wave of relief washed over me. I felt liberated, excited to be single again, and free from the constraints of a relationship. The prospect of enjoying life without any limitations or commitments was exhilarating. I was determined to dive headfirst into this newfound freedom, embracing the fun and excitement that awaited me, unencumbered by anyone else's feelings or expectations.

I frequently attended numerous clubs and house parties during that time. I vividly recall countless nights when I indulged in alcohol, drinking so much that I lost all my inhibitions. The mornings after these wild parties were often a blur, with me waking up to friends and strangers recounting my actions from the previous night. Their horrified expressions and shocked stories left me feeling deeply ashamed and embarrassed. It was as if I transformed into a completely different person under the influence, and the thought of not remembering my actions filled me with unease and anxiety.

Despite the embarrassment, I refused to let it hinder my pursuit of what I desired. I continued to party relentlessly, seeking out different guys and hooking up with them, hoping to find a meaningful connection while avoiding any commitment. I was oblivious to the potential harm my actions could cause. My primary focus was on the attention I received from men, which I craved more than anything else.

Despite the chaos in my personal life, I found solace in the stability of my work. At 21, I was promoted to restaurant manager—a significant achievement that elevated my confidence to new heights. Thriving in my role, I upgraded my wardrobe to reflect my success. Every two weeks, I visited the mall to purchase new suits, aiming to present a professional image. Wearing a well-tailored suit symbolized my accomplishments, providing an extra boost of confidence and reinforcing my sense of pride in my career.

During that time, I entered a new relationship with a colleague. We started as friends and gradually developed a close bond. Despite a significant age difference—he was 16 years older—I was drawn to his stability and maturity. Being around him made me feel safe and secure, something I had longed for in my previous relationships.

We spent much time together, and Six Flags became our special place. We would spend hours enjoying all the thrilling rides and attractions the park offered. Every visit felt like an escape to a different world, free from the stresses and worries of daily life. It was a place where I could let loose and have fun without a care in the world.

Despite our relationship's stability, significant issues hindered our progress. One of the most challenging problems was my partner's ex, who lived with him. They were trying to co-parent their child effectively, and this situation meant I was unable to visit his home. We could only spend time together during the day, which made things difficult.

I was still very much into the nightlife scene, and my partner's absence at night provided the perfect excuse to continue partying. However, this led to frequent arguments about his ex and my late-night escapades.

At the time, I knew I wasn't ready for a serious relationship. My past experiences made it difficult for me to commit. The constant coming and going of men, including father figures, left me anxious about committing and then being abandoned.

We were together for around two years, but the arguments persisted, and he couldn't give me the attention I craved. After much thought, I decided to end the relationship. Around the same time, I quit my job as a restaurant manager and started working as a bartender in a hotel. This career change gave me more time to focus on my studies, which had taken a backseat due to the demands of my previous job. Despite the difficulties, I knew that breaking up and making this career move was the right decision for me.

As a bartender, I felt right at home in the lively and social environment—the thrill of watching people unwind and let loose fulfilled me. I took immense pride in being the one who got the party started. Whether I was mixing up a classic cocktail or crafting a new creation, the satisfaction and enjoyment on my customers' faces brought me joy.

My shifts were filled with energy and excitement. The bar constantly buzzed with conversation and laughter, and I thrived in this dynamic atmosphere. I enjoyed getting to know the regulars, hearing their stories, and participating in their nightly routines. The camaraderie and connections I built with my customers were an unexpected bonus of the job.

The skills I developed as a bartender also boosted my confidence. I became adept at managing the fast-paced demands of the bar, multitasking with ease, and handling the occasional demanding customer with grace. This role allowed me to showcase my talents and gain recognition for my hard work and dedication.

While working at the hotel, I had the pleasure of meeting various interesting individuals. When I was 23, I reconnected with a guy from high school, and he quickly became my boyfriend. Unfortunately, our relationship didn't last long, as I developed feelings for another co-worker. This new guy was incredibly charming and funny, always making me laugh. Despite being in a relationship at the time, I found myself drawn to him and unable to resist his advances due to the excitement and attention he gave me.

Without much thought, I quickly ended the relationship with the first co-worker and started a relationship with the man who had been pursuing me. At first, everything seemed to be going great. We enjoyed each other's company, and I was thrilled by the passion and excitement he brought into my life. However, as time passed, I began to notice inconsistencies. He never allowed me to visit his house and could only spend limited time with me. I couldn't understand why he would pursue me so passionately if he couldn't fully commit to being with me.

As our relationship progressed, his behavior toward me began to change. He started speaking to me condescendingly and making comments that belittled me. He was always finding reasons to criticize me and point out my flaws. Even small mistakes or insignificant things allowed him to put me down. These constant jabs left me feeling inadequate and worthless as if I could never meet his expectations.

I had a strong need for validation and acceptance from men. It felt like their approval was the only thing that could make me feel worthy. Enduring this emotional abuse left me feeling rejected and unwanted. I realized that my entire life revolved around pleasing men and being desired by them. At some point, I had made them the center of my universe.

I was still heavily involved in the party scene during this period and often clubbed with my friends. I went out almost every night of the week, which my partner was unhappy about. He felt that my partying was taking a toll on our relationship and that I was not being modest. Despite his concerns, I continued to indulge in the nightlife, leading to further strain on our relationship. By then, I had grown numb and didn't care about his opinion.

After a year of dating, I mustered up the courage to end the relationship. Following the breakup, I felt empty and unworthy of love. Coping with the emotional distress of the relationship's aftermath was a significant challenge, and I struggled to find my footing. Despite the pain, I refused to give up on the hope of finding love and continued to date.

During this time, I met the lawyer who would eventually sexually assault me, which left me feeling jaded, and I began to hold onto feelings of resentment and hatred toward men.

I carried a lot of anger and sadness inside me for a long time, but I never reached out for help to deal with the emotional turmoil I was going through. Despite all the difficulties, I still felt the need for male companionship and thought that having 'friends with benefits' would be a good idea. I knew it wouldn't substitute for a real emotional connection, but it seemed like a practical option to satisfy my need for physical intimacy.

I casually dated for around a year, but I was struggling with feelings of brokenness and insecurity. I longed for love and respect from the men I met, and I believed that offering them my body was the solution to winning their hearts. I attempted to create a more profound connection with them through physical intimacy.

After my breakup with my ex, I found myself in a situation where I had to continue working with him. Initially, it was a bit awkward since we had ended things on a sour note, but as time passed, we started talking more frequently and eventually began to reconnect.

During one of our conversations, he confided in me and shared some personal struggles he had been dealing with. These struggles had caused him to be distant in our relationship, which led to our breakup. However, his honesty and vulnerability moved me and made me realize that he was genuinely remorseful. I later learned that he had taken steps to address the issues that had caused our breakup. As a result, I quickly returned to him.

After several noncommittal relationships, I had grown tired of lacking depth and yearned for something more meaningful.

Getting back with my ex would be the best option since we already had a history together. However, as our relationship progressed, I noticed things mainly stayed the same. My boyfriend was still critical of me, and it seemed he didn't have much time to spend with me.

I was disappointed because I had hoped things would be different this time. I felt like I was back to square one—stuck in a relationship that didn't fulfill my needs. I wasn't sure about our relationship's future, and I felt incredibly broken and desperate for a solution.

I believed that if I tried harder and went the extra mile, he would finally see how much I loved him and treat me better. The first thing I did was go to a jewelry store and pick out an engagement ring, thinking that if I asked for his hand in marriage, it would be the ultimate proof of my love and commitment. I hoped an engagement would be a turning point in our relationship, eliminate the mistreatment, and bring us closer together. I imagined that we would be able to build a happy future together, filled with love and mutual respect.

From the moment I decided to propose to my sweetheart, I wanted everything to be perfect. It was an essential step in our relationship, and I wanted to make it unforgettable. I spent days planning every little detail, from the location to the timing to the room's decoration.

Finally, the day arrived, and I rented a nice hotel room with a beautiful city view. I carefully arranged the rose petals I had bought all over the floor, creating a path leading to the bed, where I had arranged heart-shaped petals. I placed candles throughout the room to create a warm and romantic atmosphere, with a scent of vanilla in the air. I knew his favorite wine and made sure to have it in the room, chilling to perfection. I set the lighting to a dim and cozy level and played soft and romantic music in the background.

As I waited for him to arrive, my heart raced with excitement, and I felt nothing could stop me from asking him to be mine forever. I rehearsed the words I was going to say over and over again, making sure I got everything right.

When he arrived, he was shocked. He had no idea what was happening, and the look on his face was priceless. My love was touched that I had done all of that for him. I remember telling him I had a surprise for him, then getting on one knee and asking for his hand in marriage. He was in disbelief and said yes. His response was confirmation that I had made the right decision. Why would he say yes if he didn't love and respect me?

After that fantastic night, I felt like I was floating in the air. I had hoped it would significantly impact how he perceived and treated me, but unfortunately, that wasn't the case. I was surprised and slightly disappointed, but I put in even more effort to try and win him over.

For one of my partner's birthdays, I wanted to make it a day he would never forget. I decided to go all out and spare no expense. I went to Macy's and picked out a pair of high-quality linen pants and a Polo shirt that I knew he would love. To top it off, I got him a pair of expensive sunglasses that would look great on him.

But that was just the beginning. I planned a special night for him and wanted him to feel like a king in every way. I booked a luxurious hotel room with all the amenities, and I even got him his favorite cake from a specialty bakery.

For dinner, I made reservations at an upscale Chinese restaurant we had meant to try. The food was terrific, and we enjoyed every bite.

I also wanted to do something special for my boyfriend during Christmas to show him how much I cared about him. I decided to finance a pair of earrings worth $1600 as a gift. When he arrived to receive the gift, I eagerly awaited his reaction. However, he came empty-handed and without any gifts, which devastated me. I had been doing so much for him, trying to earn his love and affection, but the more I tried, the more I felt like a fool.

Despite my disappointment, he was in awe of the lavish gift I had given him and left with a smile. We had planned to spend New Year's Eve together, and I was excited about the prospect of entering the new year as a couple. I had even planned for us to get married that year.

He had promised to plan the celebration, and I eagerly awaited his arrival at my house. However, as the clock struck midnight and we entered 2011, he still had not arrived. I tried calling him several times, but he never answered his phone. I spent the entire night devastated and crying.

The following day, he finally contacted me and explained that he couldn't come to my house due to an emergency. However, he didn't reveal what that emergency was. At that point, I felt angry and frustrated with him. I asked him to return the earrings and ended the relationship. Despite ending things, I still hoped he would change his heart and learn to love me, but unfortunately, it never happened. Months after the incident, I cut off all communication with him and moved on with my life.

After working as a bartender for several years, I changed careers and entered the banking world. It was a significant shift in my life, and I was excited about it. However, it also meant that I would no longer be working with my ex-boyfriend, which made it easier for me to move on from him.

After the heartbreak, I became disillusioned with men and felt hesitant to trust anyone again. In my attempt to move on, I started dating multiple people in succession, hoping to find someone who could make me forget about my past. However, I made sure to be careful not to get too close to any one man, like I had with my ex. I was determined to avoid making the same mistakes again.

CHAPTER 4

TILL DEATH DO US PART?

For countless women, the idea of their wedding day is a cherished dream nurtured from a young age. Many girls delight in playing dress-up in imaginary wedding dresses, borrowing their mother's jewelry to complete their look. As they age, these fantasies become more detailed and specific, with visions of the perfect romantic location and decor taking center stage. They might start creating mood boards, scrapbooks, or Pinterest boards to capture their inspirations and ideas.

The dream wedding day is often seen as a once-in-a-lifetime event, meticulously planned down to the smallest detail. Every aspect is considered, from the number of guests to the choice of music and cuisine. The atmosphere is carefully crafted to create a romantic and unforgettable experience that will be remembered for years. Many women spend countless hours researching and planning every element of their wedding day, from the perfect flowers to the ideal lighting and the most stunning decor, ensuring that their vision is brought to life in the most magical way possible.

Throughout my childhood, marriage was rarely discussed in my family. It was never emphasized as an important milestone or goal. Instead, my strongest desire was companionship. Loneliness often overshadowed my life, and I yearned for someone to share my time with, someone who would understand and be there for me. Dating became my primary means of seeking this special connection to fill the void I felt so deeply.

When I proposed to my ex-partner, it wasn't because I was driven by a desire to marry. My motivation stemmed from a deep need for attention and the fear of being alone. I was desperate to hold on to someone who could provide me the companionship I longed for. Unfortunately, our relationship didn't last, and I found myself single once again, grappling with feelings of rejection and loss.

After the breakup, my fixation on finding true love intensified. I went on numerous dates, hoping to meet someone who shared my desire for a serious, committed relationship. However, time and again, I was met with disappointment. None of the men I met were looking for the same depth of connection that I was. This constant cycle of hope and disillusionment left me feeling shattered, disheartened, and worthless as if there was something inherently wrong with me that made me unworthy of love and respect.

This relentless quest for a partner who would cherish and value me consumed my thoughts and actions. I longed for someone who would see me for who I was and treat me with the love and respect I believed I deserved. In the meantime, I remained heavily involved in the party scene. It was an environment where I could meet men and momentarily escape my feelings of inadequacy. Despite knowing the negative consequences of excessive partying, I couldn't resist the allure of male attention. My self-esteem was so low that I relied on compliments from others to feel worthy. Without external validation, I felt incomplete.

During Christmas of 2010, the bank where I worked organized a holiday outing at a restaurant. We had a wonderful time talking and laughing over our meal. After dinner, some of my co-workers and I decided to continue the celebration at a club. The atmosphere was lively and vibrant, and we ordered drinks to enjoy the night. While dancing with one of my co-workers, a handsome man approached me. He was medium height with a stunning, rich brown complexion that looked even more beautiful under the club lights. His face was adorned with an enchanting smile, and his dimples added to his charm.

We started a conversation, and I felt an instant connection with him. We spoke for several minutes before he asked for my number. I was thrilled because I had a gut feeling that he was different from the others I had met. As we left the club, we continued our conversation over the phone for hours. That one night, I felt myself falling for him. He made me feel special and cared for as if I were the only person who mattered to him. His sweet words and gentle tone made my heart skip a beat. Right then, I knew this was someone I wanted to spend more time with and get to know better.

He had a young child, which made it challenging for us to spend as much time together as we would have liked. Despite this, he always made a conscious effort to carve out quality time for us whenever possible. His dedication to balancing parental responsibilities with our relationship made me feel genuinely valued and loved. For the first time, I could envision a future with someone, and the idea of marrying him began to feel like a genuine possibility.

After being in a relationship for three months, we decided it was time for me to meet his child. I was incredibly nervous because I had never met anyone's child before. I wanted to make a good impression and understood this was a crucial step in our relationship. It was essential to show the child that I was someone they could trust and look up to. This responsibility felt significant, but I was honored to have the opportunity to influence her life positively. This realization prompted me to look closer at my lifestyle and habits. I understood that engaging in non-productive activities and going out multiple times a week would not set a good example for the child.

After dating for six months, my partner and I decided to move in together. This was an exciting milestone but also made me anxious, as it was my first time living with a guy. Moving in together also meant I would help care for his child. Although her mother was still involved in her life, I was expected to support her upbringing. This new responsibility was daunting, but I was eager to embrace it and do my best to help raise the child with love, care, and attention.

In the beginning, our life together was everything I had always dreamed of. We cherished each other's company and made it a priority to spend quality time together every day. Coming home to him after a long day at work filled me with joy and anticipation. The comfort and warmth of our home only added to this happiness.

Our connection was deep, and we were enthusiastic about building a future together. We shared our desires, ambitions, and goals, experiencing a sense of satisfaction I had never felt in my previous relationships. It felt like I had finally found my soulmate, and I had no desire to escape this beautiful relationship we had built together. Every day was filled with excitement, and I was thrilled about what the future held for us.

As we grew closer, we knew our next step was to get married. We initially planned to tie the knot in October 2012, and the thought of a grand wedding ceremony filled me with immense joy. I chose ten of my closest friends as my bridesmaids and selected a maid of honor. Our wedding colors were to be burnt orange and cream, perfectly matching the autumn season. I even asked a friend to make our wedding cake. Everything seemed perfect, and I couldn't wait to start this new chapter of our lives together.

But as it often happens, life had other plans for us. Unforeseen circumstances arose, and my mother fell ill. Her condition worsened quickly, and it became clear that we would have to move the wedding date to May of the same year. Although I was deeply disappointed that my dream wedding would have to be postponed, nothing was more important to us than having my mother by our side on our special day. We knew we couldn't proceed with the wedding without her and were determined to ensure she could attend.

My mother had been dealing with heart issues for years, and she had recently been diagnosed with congestive heart failure. The news was devastating, and I had no idea how long she had to live. However, her presence at my wedding was something I couldn't imagine ever compromising on.

We decided to have a courthouse wedding instead. Some people were against the idea, thinking that a church wedding with a pastor would be more appropriate. However, I didn't care where we got married at that time. I barely went to church, and my only concern was for my mother to be able to attend my wedding.

Before getting married, my fiancé officially proposed to me in front of my mom and aunt. It was like a scene from a fairytale. I felt like a princess, a feeling I had always craved. It was the first time I had ever felt truly worthy of love.

On my wedding day, I was filled with an overwhelming sense of happiness. It was hard to believe that this day had finally arrived. I had never really pictured myself as a married woman. I didn't think it was on the cards for me. But here I was, about to embark on a journey with the love of my life, and I couldn't be more excited.

We got married at the courthouse on a beautiful Friday afternoon. The intimate ceremony made the occasion all the more special. The simplicity of the setting allowed us to focus on the significance of the moment rather than the event's grandeur. The following day, we held our reception at a cozy restaurant. The atmosphere was warm and inviting, and being surrounded by family and friends made it all the more meaningful.

The entire experience was nothing short of a dream. We laughed and celebrated our union with those we loved most. The highlight was that my mother was there to witness everything. Her presence was a testament to her strength and love; having her by my side on my wedding day was a dream come true.

At the beginning of our union, our marriage was breathtaking. Being addressed as a wife and calling someone my husband brought an indescribable amount of happiness and fulfillment to my life. I also had the added responsibility of being a stepmom, which I took very seriously. I focused on setting a good example for my stepchild and ensuring she felt loved and supported in every possible way.

For about a year, everything was great. However, as time passed, the initial excitement and thrill of being married faded. It was then that I began to notice how unprepared we were for this new phase of life. I had never thought about what it meant to be a wife, nor had I sought guidance from God or women in successful marriages.

As I navigated through my new role, I realized that all the trauma I had endured in my past had followed me into my marriage. Trusting men was still a foreign concept to me, and this lack of trust made me try to control everything in my marriage. I was also very opinionated and would often start arguments over small things.

I didn't view my husband as an equal partner in our marriage but more like a child who needed my guidance. Instead of supporting and encouraging him, I often criticized and pointed out his mistakes. I believed our financial situation was stagnant because of his lack of ambition, and I would blame him. I made more money than he did and wanted him to surpass me and be the breadwinner. I failed to realize that my constant belittling and negativity towards him likely contributed to his lack of motivation. This mindset made me feel more dominant and less feminine, which in turn negatively impacted my sex drive.

In my marriage, I slowly lost interest because it didn't match the ideal relationship I had envisioned. I was seeking a partner who would be my knight in shining armor and help me heal from all my past traumas and fill in the gaps left by my father figures and previous relationships. However, I often felt disappointed because my partner could not fulfill all my needs. I used to observe happy and successful marriages from a distance and believed that their happiness resulted from having no issues or challenges to face. Therefore, when my marriage was met with various problems and obstacles, I immediately assumed that it meant we were not meant to be together.

I had been in several relationships that didn't last, so when I got married, I found it challenging to understand what it meant to be in a covenant. As time passed, I felt less connected to my husband—we seemed to be growing apart. I began to feel restless and looked at other men, hoping to find that connection missing in my marriage. I started romanticizing the idea of a perfect relationship without flaws, forgetting that every relationship has its challenges.

Our communication began to suffer as a result. I often shut down during disagreements, avoiding meaningful conversations that could have helped resolve our issues. My expectations and the reality of our marriage clashed, leading to frustration and disappointment. I began feeling isolated in my home, surrounded by unresolved feelings and unmet expectations.

On my 30th birthday in 2014, my husband surprised me by throwing a birthday party. It was a thoughtful gesture, but at that point, I was already emotionally checked out of the relationship. Despite his efforts, I couldn't shake the feeling that something was missing between us.

My husband asked one of my co-workers and some of her friends to help with the preparations. They had a friend who was a baker, and they recommended that he make the cake for the party. The baker brought the cake himself, and he was encouraged to stay for a while. As the night progressed, I found myself becoming increasingly attracted to him. I couldn't help but notice how alluring he was, with his easy charm and confident demeanor. We exchanged numbers under the pretense of hiring him for other upcoming events, but we had undeniable chemistry.

Despite the attraction, I didn't think anything would happen between us. After all, I was married. However, one day, feeling particularly lonely and disconnected from my husband, I texted the baker and started a conversation. To my surprise, we had a great chat that turned into several engaging discussions. I found myself eagerly looking forward to our talks and feeling excited about the possibility of getting to know him better. Our conversations soon turned into an affair that lasted about two weeks. I wanted a relationship, but he decided it was not a good idea. At that time, I was focused on what I wanted and felt rejected when he didn't reciprocate.

After the infidelity towards the end of 2014, my life took a turn for the worse. I began to experience the symptoms of rheumatoid arthritis, and to my surprise, co-workers and others who were close to me started to change their attitudes toward me. I adopted a victim mindset, feeling that everyone was unjustified in their treatment of me. I didn't feel guilty about the affair at the time because I had always been used to hopping from one relationship to the next, treating my marriage like just another relationship.

In 2015, I found myself in several situations where I couldn't believe how terrible my life had become. It seemed like anything that could go wrong did. From personal relationships to work-related issues, I constantly struggled to keep my head above water. Despite my best efforts, my situation worsened as the year went on.

During that year, my husband and I faced a challenging situation where we realized it was better for us to part ways. I had checked out of the marriage and couldn't see myself checking back in. I didn't know then that he had met someone else and believed that pursuing a relationship with her was the right choice. It was difficult for both of us, as we had invested much time and emotion in our marriage.

The realization that our marriage was over was heartbreaking. We had shared dreams, hopes, and plans for the future, all of which seemed to crumble around us. The emotional distance that had grown between us over the years now seemed insurmountable. I felt a mixture of sadness, anger, and regret, questioning how we had reached this point and what could have been done differently.

The process of separating our lives was painful and complicated. We had to untangle not just our emotional bond but also our shared responsibilities and possessions. The experience was overwhelming, and I often felt lost and alone. The comfort and familiarity of our life together were gone, replaced by uncertainty and fear about the future.

During this tumultuous time, I struggled to find my footing. The weight of my mistakes and the consequences of my actions bore down on me. I realized that my pattern of seeking validation and jumping from one relationship to another had ultimately led to my downfall.

The separation left me feeling numb and lost. The overwhelming sense of loneliness and despair was unlike anything I had ever experienced before. I felt adrift in a sea of confusion, unsure of what to do next or how to cope with the intense emotional pain. Every day felt like an impossible challenge, and I struggled to find even the slightest glimmer of hope.

The depths of my depression became so severe that I began contemplating the unthinkable. One day at work, I found myself researching how many anxiety pills it would take to end my life. I had been prescribed the medication for my chronic anxiety, and after reading the dosage information, I realized I had more than enough to carry out my plan.

That same day, consumed by a sense of hopelessness and desperation, I went into an office at work with a plan to take enough medication to end it all. I had never felt depression of such magnitude before, and the weight of my sorrow was crushing. I started by taking seven pills, intending to take more.

But then, in that moment of darkness, I heard a clear and unmistakable voice that I believed was God—telling me to stop. The command was so powerful and immediate that it broke through the haze of my despair. It was like a lifeline had been thrown to me just as I was about to slip beneath the surface.

Acting on this divine intervention, I immediately texted one of my friends who worked with me. My message was a cry for help, and within moments, the entire staff came rushing to my aid. Their concern and support were overwhelming, and it was clear that they would not let me face this alone.

Not knowing for sure how many pills I had taken, my manager called 911. Paramedics arrived quickly, and I was rushed to the hospital. Thankfully, the only side effect I experienced was drowsiness. I found myself dozing off during the trip to the hospital, feeling a strange mix of relief and exhaustion. When I woke up, a chaplain was praying over me. I wasn't used to anyone praying for me, but in that moment, it was incredibly comforting and exactly what I needed.

Realizing the gravity of my mental health crisis, I made the voluntary decision to check myself into a mental institution for four days. During my stay, I focused entirely on my recovery. The environment was safe and supportive, providing a much-needed refuge from the turmoil of my everyday life. I worked closely with the medical staff, following a structured treatment plan designed to help me address my mental health issues and regain some semblance of stability.

My primary goal was to get back to my routine with a renewed sense of confidence and stability. I knew that healing wouldn't happen overnight, but I was determined to take the necessary steps toward recovery. Each day in the institution brought new insights and small victories, and I gradually felt more like myself again.

After being released, my husband picked me up from the institution. I was hopeful that this experience might bring us closer together, providing an opportunity for reconciliation. However, to my dismay, he was very cold and distant. It was as if he harbored a deep resentment toward me. He drove me home quickly, barely speaking to me, and dropped me off. His behavior left me devastated and feeling utterly alone in the world.

To cope with the pain of separation and the overwhelming sense of isolation, I decided to start dating again. A new relationship could help me move on from the past and bring excitement and joy back into my life. I wanted a fresh start and to feel loved and appreciated once more. Dating seemed like a way to achieve that—a way to fill a void left by my failed marriage and begin a new chapter in my life.

During the period of separation from my husband, I decided to try online dating as a way to meet new people without the added stress of going out to socialize. I entered into two separate relationships, each lasting around six months. While these relationships provided temporary comfort and companionship, they were also a blur because I felt like I was losing my mind. After these relationships ended, I sought new connections by traveling to different states to meet men I had met through online dating. Despite the risks and challenges associated with this approach, I found it was a way to try and escape my miserable life.

One of the men I met online lived in Pennsylvania. After exchanging a few messages and having a couple of conversations over the phone, I decided to take a chance and drive to meet him. The drive was long, but I was finally excited to meet him in person.

The first couple of days with him were extraordinary. He took me on a tour of the area, showing me some of the most beautiful spots. We visited several great restaurants and tried delicious food. His knowledge of the area and eagerness to show me around impressed me.

He even took me to a house under renovation and told me it would be our new home. I was overjoyed at the thought of starting a fresh life with him in Pennsylvania. The house was stunning, and I could easily envision us living there and creating a future together.

During my visit, I noticed several pill bottles lying open on the table, with pills scattered around. Concerned, I asked him about it. That's when he opened up to me and revealed that he had bipolar disorder. He assured me that he was taking his medication and that his condition was under control. He was calm and composed when he said this, so I didn't think much of it.

I had the chance to spend two beautiful days with him, filled with meaningful conversations, shared experiences, and enjoyable company. However, I had to return to Maryland for a job interview. I had lost my previous job due to the drama I had caused at work. Everyone knew about my infidelity and suicide attempt, and I also had trouble concentrating and missed many days. Despite the job loss, I was excited about the interview and the possibility of starting a new chapter in my life.

After the interview, I drove back to Pennsylvania excitedly, looking forward to sharing the news with him. However, when I arrived, I noticed his mood had changed entirely. He was visibly angry and started yelling at me without any explanation. I was shocked and confused, wondering what had happened while I was away.

His aggressive behavior caused me to fear for my safety. Realizing I needed to leave immediately, I gathered my belongings quickly. With my heart racing, I ran out of his house and jumped into my car. I drove away as fast as possible, trying to put as much distance between us as possible.

While driving home, I called another guy I had met online. We had several conversations, and I felt we were developing a friendship. I told him about the incident, and he insisted I come to his house. So, that night, I drove for approximately four hours from Pennsylvania to Virginia. I felt safe going to his house because he had an older female roommate. When I reached his home, we talked briefly in his room. He then laid me on the bed and began kissing me. After that, he started removing my clothes. I was uncomfortable with what was happening but afraid to tell him no. He then laid on top of me and began having intercourse with me. I wanted him to stop and told him no, but he would not move.

As I opened my eyes the following day, I felt a sense of numbness wash over me. It was as if my body had given up on feeling anything after the emotional rollercoaster I had been on. Memories of the previous night came flooding back to me, and I couldn't help but feel overwhelmed. The pain, the anger, the confusion—it was all too much. I knew I had to leave his house and escape it all. So, I gathered my things, quietly slipped out of the room, and headed towards my car. As I drove back home, my mind was filled with thoughts of what had happened, and I wondered how I would ever be able to handle it all. That same day, the man from Pennsylvania called me and told me that he was going to find me, chop me up into pieces, and throw me into the river. I didn't go to the police because I didn't care anymore.

During that period, I was struggling with my emotions and found myself in a very dark place. Despite feeling lost and overwhelmed, I kept dating because I believed finding the right person would improve everything. For the rest of 2015 and part of 2016, I didn't pay much attention to whether or not the men I dated were compatible with me. I approached dating with detachment, not caring if these men were meant to be a part of my life. I realize I was trying to fill a void, but unfortunately, my approach to dating only caused more confusion and heartache.

In July 2016, I reconnected with a guy I went to grade school with, which was a pleasant surprise. I felt lonely and disconnected; talking to him was like a breath of fresh air. After reconnecting, we started dating quickly, and I found him to be kind, genuine, and trustworthy. I felt safe around him and knew he was different from the most recent men.

A month after we started our relationship, we received the heartbreaking news that my mother was dying. It was devastating for me and my family. I had already spent my life without my father, and now I was going to lose my mother, too. The news hit me like a ton of bricks, and I felt emotionless. I didn't know how to cope with the reality of her illness, so I started to distance myself from her. I believed that if I detached myself emotionally from her, it would make it easier for me to handle her loss when it eventually happened.

My mom was my best friend, and the thought of losing her was unbearable. I felt like I was losing a part of myself, and I didn't know how to live without her. I tried to keep myself busy with work and other activities, but nothing seemed to help. I was going through the motions, pretending everything was okay, when I was falling apart inside.

In October 2016, I lost my mother, which was a challenging time for me. I spent her last days in the hospital by her side, and watching her slowly slip away and drift off into a coma, never to wake up again, was a surreal and heartbreaking experience. The pain I felt was so intense that, at first, I tried to numb it and push it away. Unfortunately, the same month saw the finalization of my divorce, which left me feeling like scum, utterly lost, and alone. I didn't know how to cope with all the pain and sadness, so I turned to smoking weed and alcohol as a way to numb my emotions.

I was fortunate enough to have my boyfriend by my side during the most challenging time of my life. He was always there for me whenever I needed him, lending me an empathetic ear, offering comfort, and supporting me in every way possible. I can't imagine how I would have made it through without him.

When my mother became ill, I spent seven years preparing for the worst. I thought I had mentally braced myself for her eventual passing, but I was mistaken. The grief and sorrow that followed were far more intense than anything I could have ever imagined. It was like repeatedly hitting rock bottom, and I felt I had nothing to give.

Despite my boyfriend's unwavering support and efforts to assist me, my pain persisted, gnawing away at my spirit. I felt lost, hopeless, and utterly without direction in life. For most of my adult years, I had been a lukewarm Christian, never deeply engaged with my faith, and seldom considered seeking God's help during tough times. Eventually, I even stopped believing in Jesus after my boyfriend convinced me that He was not real. It was easy for me to abandon my faith because I harbored the belief that God had taken my mother away from me as a punishment for my adultery.

Turning away from my faith led me down an even darker path than the one I was already on. I began to harbor deep-seated negative feelings towards Jesus and sought solace in the New Age movement. I hoped that psychics, affirmations, chakras, and meditation would fill the void that I felt God had failed to fill. I believed that by immersing myself in these practices, I would finally find the peace and purpose I had been desperately searching for. However, I soon realized that these temporary fixes did not bring me the inner peace and fulfillment I truly desired.

As I distanced myself from my faith, I also began to resent my boyfriend, despite knowing it was my personal decision to abandon my beliefs. I found myself blaming him for my spiritual void. This resentment only added to my emotional turmoil, leaving me in a confusing and turbulent state where I felt disconnected from everything and everyone. It was as if I were enveloped in a bubble of anger and negativity, easily provoked by the most minor things. My temper became short, and I lashed out indiscriminately, not caring who bore the brunt of my anger.

Refusing to acknowledge God's existence, I relied solely on my strength. The pain of losing my mom was still deeply ingrained in me, but I was convinced nothing that God could do would fit it. The mere mention of Jesus repulsed me, and I would roll my eyes whenever someone invited me to church. I often spent days in bed, crying over the perceived purposelessness of my life. I hated my job, felt unhappy in my relationship, and saw no hope for a better future. The darkness of my despair seemed impenetrable, and I couldn't see a way out. Thoughts of suicide constantly plagued me, yet I was too terrified to act on them.

During my four-year relationship, my feelings towards my partner fluctuated constantly. Some days, I felt an intense desire to be with him because he was my boyfriend and best friend, someone I couldn't imagine my life without. Yet, there were also days when I felt an overwhelming urge to run away from the relationship.

Whenever I felt the need to leave, I reminded myself of the countless times he had supported me through difficult moments and celebrated my successes. Despite my wavering feelings, he was always a steady source of safety and comfort.

By 2019, after being together for three years, I found myself emotionally checked out. At that time, my boyfriend, brother, and I lived together in a townhouse we had moved into two years earlier. While the arrangement was comfortable, something about it no longer felt right.

Around the same time, my 24-year-old cousin decided to move in with us. He was looking to get his life in order, planning to earn his GED and find a good job. I was glad to have him with us, seeing it as an opportunity for him to get back on his feet.

Tragically, only a month after moving in, my cousin died. In August 2019, his mother picked him up to help with groceries. I remember saying goodbye, expecting to see him later. Instead, a few hours later, my brother called with devastating news: my cousin had died of a heart attack in his mother's arms. His death at just 24, as he was trying so hard to rebuild his life, hit me harder than losing my mother.

My cousin and I, despite being ten years apart in age, shared a close bond and lived together for a time when we first moved to Maryland. He was more than just a cousin to me; he was like a brother, one of the kindest souls you could ever meet. His untimely passing left me grappling with intense anger towards God. How could He take away someone who was on the brink of turning their life around? The pain was unbearable, overshadowing any thoughts of leaving my boyfriend as I was consumed with grief.

On December 1st, I found out I was pregnant. Initially, I was shocked and overwhelmed with fear. Although I was unhappy in my relationship, I felt I had to marry my boyfriend for the sake of our unborn child. I had always dreamed of having a family and didn't want my child to grow up in a broken home. Despite knowing my boyfriend would be a great father, I couldn't shake the feeling that something was off.

In late December 2019, I suffered a miscarriage. It was a devastating blow, yet it felt like just another addition to my already overwhelming list of traumas. I struggled to prioritize my feelings and emotions, constantly dealing with so much pain and sorrow.

A week after my miscarriage, I became severely ill. As the new year began, I found myself frequently in and out of the hospital, with no doctor able to diagnose my condition. My health deteriorated to the point where I had to leave my job, focusing solely on trying to get better.

In 2018, I enrolled in a program to become an integrative health and wellness coach, which I completed in 2019. This experience gave me the wisdom and tools to transform my health and help others improve theirs. I learned to eliminate harmful foods from my diet and sought the expertise of a functional medicine doctor. In 2020 I was diagnosed with Ehlers-Danlos Hypermobility Syndrome and Rheumatoid Arthritis. These diagnoses, while severe, motivated me to prioritize my health.

Amidst my health journey, the COVID-19 pandemic struck. While dealing with my illness, the pandemic provided an unexpected opportunity to focus entirely on my well-being. I stayed home throughout the year and launched my health and wellness business with the help of a marketing team. I felt a sense of purpose for the first time in a long while. My business began to attract clients who achieved remarkable results, which fueled my passion and drive. Despite this success, I had yet to discover faith in Jesus.

With my newfound purpose, I experienced a surge of confidence that had been absent for a long time. Over the course of a year, I lost nearly 60 pounds and successfully established a thriving business. This boost in self-assurance reignited my desire to start dating again. Although I had been in a relationship with my then-boyfriend for almost four years, I realized it was time to move on and find someone who shared my values and passions.

In August 2020, I gathered the courage to end my relationship and ventured into the dating world again. I went on several dates, hoping to find someone who would understand and support my goals and aspirations. This new chapter was exciting and daunting as I sought a partner aligned with my newfound confidence and purpose.

In November 2020, I noticed a man who had commented on one of my health and wellness posts. Intrigued by his words, I checked his social media profile and discovered that he frequently discussed the Bible and Jesus in his posts. Although I wasn't a believer then, his religious beliefs made me feel like he would be a safe and trustworthy person to talk to.

We began chatting online, and we quickly hit it off. He seemed kind and compassionate, genuinely caring about people. Before long, our conversations moved offline, and we started spending more time together in person. He would visit me at my townhome and talk for hours about everything from our interests to our struggles.

My ex had moved out, and our lease was up in January 2021, so I knew I would need to find a new place soon. Despite the uncertainty of my living situation, I found comfort in the presence of this new man in my life. He provided stability and support when I needed it most.

While we were together one day, he suggested I move into his apartment. Initially, I was taken aback and felt a bit nervous about the idea. However, after careful consideration, I accepted his offer and moved in with him. It wasn't an easy decision, but I trusted it was the right thing to do.

At first, living with my partner was enjoyable. However, it wasn't long before we began having frequent arguments. These arguments often consumed entire days and revolved around topics like my past and the existence of Jesus. What troubled me most was his lack of trust in me. This distrust made me feel uneasy and prevented me from going places alone, leading me to spend all my time with him.

I often saw him reading his Bible, which initially annoyed me. I couldn't understand how someone could have such faith in a book written by humans. Determined to prove him wrong, I spent hours searching the internet for evidence to disprove the existence of Jesus.

During one of our conversations, he mentioned considering celibacy, a concept unfamiliar to me as no one had ever brought it up before. Despite his thoughts on celibacy, we continued to have sexual intercourse. However, he often felt guilty afterward, which started to irritate me. I didn't see anything wrong with engaging in sexual activity before marriage as long as we were in a committed and monogamous relationship. I believed we were doing what was suitable for us at the time.

After being in a relationship for four months, I began to feel a strong urge to stop having sex. I knew I needed to discuss this with my boyfriend, so I did. We agreed to refrain from sexual activity. However, even after we stopped having sex, the intensity and frequency of our arguments remained unchanged. He began to resent me for initiating our previous sexual encounters, which made me feel terrible. He did not see me as someone he could spend the rest of his life with, and this realization destroyed my self-esteem.

I had conflicting thoughts about my relationship with my partner. On one hand, I longed for him to see me as his wife and to have a fulfilling, loving relationship with him. On the other hand, the constant turmoil we experienced made me feel a strong urge to leave. The arguments, distrust, and emotional strain were becoming too much to bear. However, amidst all this emotional turmoil, something unexpected happened that changed the course of my life.

After observing my partner's consistent devotion to reading the Bible, I became increasingly curious about Jesus. I started to wonder if He was real and if there was more to the faith my partner deeply believed in. This curiosity led me to begin asking God about His existence. For two weeks, I prayed earnestly with all my heart, seeking answers and clarity.

One day, while lying on the living room floor, I asked God again if Jesus was real, and then I experienced an indescribable feeling that was entirely new to me. It was a sensation of intense warmth, peace, and love that I instinctively knew was from Jesus. This feeling was so powerful and transformative that it left me yearning for more. It felt like a light had been switched on inside me, illuminating a path I had never seen before.

Compelled by this experience, I spent hours upon hours reading the Bible, eager to learn more about God and Jesus. The more I read, the more I felt connected to a profound truth I had never known. The teachings, stories, and messages resonated deeply with me, providing comfort and answers to questions I had long pondered.

This newfound faith started to reshape my perspective on life and my relationship. I began to see things through a different lens, one that was infused with hope and purpose. Despite the ongoing challenges with my partner, this spiritual awakening gave me a sense of direction and inner peace that I had never experienced before.

CHAPTER 5

A JOURNEY OF FAITH AND DECEPTION

When I decided to give my life to Jesus, it marked a profound turning point for me. God began to show me what being His child meant, unveiling a deeper understanding of His love and purpose. I realized I had spent my entire life seeking fulfillment in all the wrong places outside God's will. In a quest to realign myself with His divine plan, I dedicated a year to isolation, immersing myself in the Bible and seeking to know Jesus more intimately. I truly fell in love with Him and His teachings during this time. The more I read and learned, the more my faith blossomed, and I began to grasp the true essence of love, forgiveness, and compassion. Giving my life to Jesus was not merely a decision but a transformative journey of rediscovering my true identity and finding my purpose in Him.

Despite my newfound faith, my relationship remained tumultuous. We spent up to eight hours a day arguing, which was emotionally draining. I had hoped that my religious conversion would change his perspective of me, but that wasn't the case.

This constant turmoil led me to a place where I felt a strong desire to be single, which was entirely new to me. I believed being single would help me develop the peace and joy I yearned for, but the fear of starting over kept me in the relationship.

As the months passed, the arguments and emotional strain became unbearable. The desire to be single grew stronger, eclipsing my fear of the unknown. I realized that staying in a toxic relationship out of fear was not the path God intended for me or him. With a heavy heart, I decided to end the relationship and move out.

For seven months, I slept in my brother's living room before finally securing my own room. Although this period was uncomfortable and uncertain, I was resolute in my obedience to God. I took a leap of faith, trusting that He would guide me through this new chapter of my life. This faith journey has been a testament to God's unwavering support and the transformative power of His love.

After breaking up with my partner, I was single for about three weeks. Initially, it was a welcome change, giving me the space to focus on myself and my personal growth. However, as time went on, I began to feel an intense sense of loneliness. This loneliness left me questioning whether being single was indeed what I wanted or if it was God's plan for me. I couldn't help but wonder if my reluctance stemmed from a fear of entering another bad relationship.

Despite my doubts, I felt three weeks was enough time to be single. Over the past year, I have grown significantly, choosing to remain celibate and focus on becoming a more virtuous person. I finally understood the importance of marriage and felt ready to apply my newfound wisdom in a new relationship.

I decided to search for men who shared a strong relationship with God on social media, as spirituality had become a crucial aspect of my life. After some browsing, I came across a man who caught my attention. He appeared passionate about his faith, maintained his own podcast, and was highly ambitious. Impressed by his qualities, I commented on one of his posts. To my surprise, he responded, and we started chatting. Despite living in a different state, I wasn't discouraged and remained open to the possibility of relocating if our relationship blossomed.

Before deciding to date again, I distinctly remember hearing God's voice telling me that the process from meeting to marriage would be quick when the right man came along. Almost instantly, I connected with a man who seemed to fit this description.

He and I hit it off immediately, and within a week of talking, he called me his soulmate. Hearing this made my heart leap with joy, and I felt God had sent him to me as my husband. We continued talking on the phone for about a month before meeting in person, during which time our connection grew even stronger.

As the day of our meeting approached, I eagerly anticipated the experience of flying to see him. I hadn't been on a plane for some time and was looking forward to it. We had arranged to stay in a hotel together, which made me slightly nervous. However, having been celibate for a year, I was confident that nothing would happen between us since we had agreed to wait until marriage.

On the day of our meeting, we were both overjoyed and ecstatic. I couldn't wait to embrace the man I knew would be my husband. The anticipation of finally being with the person I had been talking to for so long was exhilarating. I was practically jumping with joy as I made my way to the airport, eager to meet him in person.

As I walked out of the airport, my heart raced with excitement. I had been waiting for this moment for what felt like forever. And there he was, waiting for me beside his car, looking just as handsome as I had imagined. He had a tall, muscular build, and his smile was infectious. I couldn't believe that I was finally meeting him in person. It was a dream come true, and I knew this was just the beginning of an incredible journey together.

We wrapped our arms around each other in a warm and comforting embrace as soon as we met. It was as if we had known each other for years. Holding hands, we drove to the hotel, gazing at the beautiful scenery and talking excitedly. The moment felt surreal, and I was filled with a sense of peace and contentment, knowing that I was exactly where I was meant to be.

We talked for hours that first night, ranging from deep and philosophical to light and humorous. He had a way of intellectually stimulating me, challenging my thoughts and beliefs in a way that made me feel invigorated and vulnerable.

Despite my initial uneasiness, I felt safe and protected around him. There was a calming and reassuring aura about him that put me at ease. As we settled into our hotel room, the conversations flowed naturally, and I found myself laughing and sharing more than I had with anyone else in a long time. His presence made me feel secure, which helped lower my defenses and allowed me to open up more easily.

As the evening progressed, we continued discussing our dreams, faith, and plans for the future. His passion for God and his ambitions were evident, making me even more confident that he was the right person for me. The emotional connection we had built over the past month deepened as we shared more about our lives and our spiritual journeys.

However, despite my resolve to remain celibate until marriage, our physical attraction grew stronger. We found ourselves drawn to each other in an exciting and overwhelming way. The lines between our spiritual connection and physical desire blurred as the night went on.

Eventually, we succumbed to our desires and ended up having intercourse. In the immediate aftermath, a wave of conviction washed over me. I had spent the past year striving to live a life that honored God, and this moment felt like a significant deviation from that path. Yet, in my heart, I rationalized that one mistake was okay because I genuinely believed he would be my husband.

The next day, he had planned a full day of activities for us. We started by attending a sports event where his best friend's son played. Watching the game together was an enjoyable experience, and it felt like a glimpse into what our future weekends might look like. After cheering for the young athletes, we went sightseeing around the city. He took me to several iconic spots, sharing stories and little-known facts about each place.

One of the day's highlights was our visit to an art museum. I was utterly mesmerized by the beautiful artwork on display. We wandered through the different exhibits, our hands occasionally brushing against each other, and I fell deeper in love with him. His appreciation for art mirrored my own, and I could easily envision spending the rest of my life with someone who shared my passions.

As the day continued, we strolled along the boardwalk by the water, eventually making our way to a charming seafood restaurant. The ambiance was perfect, with the gentle sound of waves lapping against the shore and the setting sun casting a golden glow. Over dinner, we delved into our future plans, discussing dreams of starting a family and marriage. Each conversation brought us closer, and I felt a deep sense of alignment with his vision for the future.

The day's events concluded with a visit to meet his best friend. His friend welcomed me warmly, though with a barrage of questions aimed at getting to know me better. Despite feeling a bit jittery, I found solace in the genuine care his friend had for him. It was comforting to know that he had such supportive people in his life, and it made me feel even more secure in my feelings for him.

The evening before my departure home was filled with a profound melancholy. It was challenging to say farewell to the man with whom I had developed such strong feelings. The following morning, he accompanied me to the airport bright and early. We both struggled with the idea of parting ways, sharing lingering glances and heartfelt promises to see each other soon.

In the first week following my return home, we maintained regular video chats to explore the potential of our future together. He, being an entrepreneur, expressed a keen interest in having me join him in his business endeavors and even contemplated relocating to my state. I was sure he was the man I wanted to spend the rest of my life with. Every conversation solidified our bond, and I felt a growing certainty that we were meant to be together.

However, after a few weeks, I noticed a significant shift in his behavior. He became increasingly uncommunicative and less responsive. This sudden change left me feeling uneasy and uncertain about the future of our relationship. I couldn't comprehend what had gone wrong. We had numerous conversations about the possibility of him moving to my area, and everything seemed so promising. It was particularly painful because even my friends believed he was the right person for me.

I kept replaying what I thought was a message from God, suggesting that the right man would enter my life quickly. The confusion and heartache were overwhelming. I had believed so strongly in the promise of our future together, and now I was left grappling with the disheartening reality that things were falling apart.

The distance between us grew wider as the days turned into weeks, and his silence became more pronounced. I questioned everything—my decisions, my faith, and the path I thought God had laid out for me. It was a difficult and painful period of introspection, but I knew I had to trust in God's plan, even if it wasn't unfolding as I envisioned.

I eventually stopped talking to him. At this point, I was desperate to find a husband. I started searching on social media and found another guy whose posts showed a deep love for God. His words resonated deeply with me, and I regularly liked his posts. It wasn't long before he noticed me and sent a friendly message expressing his gratitude for my support. Our initial exchanges were lighthearted and filled with mutual admiration for each other's faith.

After exchanging messages for a few hours, he asked for my phone number. We began talking on the phone, and I soon learned more about his life. He mentioned that he owned a chain of funeral homes, a family business he was passionate about. His satisfaction and dedication were evident, and I couldn't help but feel excited when he talked about the possibility of us running the business together one day.

He mentioned that his mother and father were devoted followers of Jesus and had been married for over 30 years. This intrigued me because I hadn't encountered such strong religious devotion in a family before, and I admired them as role models for a successful marriage.

As our conversations deepened, he shared more about his entrepreneurial endeavors. In addition to the funeral homes, he also bought repossessed cars at auctions and resold them for a profit. His voice brimmed with enthusiasm as he detailed the process, and I found myself intrigued by the opportunity. He seemed genuine and trustworthy, and his business acumen impressed me.

After a week of talking on the phone, he proposed an investment opportunity. He suggested I invest $1,800 to purchase a repossessed car, promising substantial returns once the vehicle was sold. His proposition seemed like a safe and lucrative venture, and I trusted him. Without much hesitation, I transferred the money to him, excited about the potential profits and the prospect of being involved in his business.

After investing, he continued to involve me in his business plans, sharing updates and including me in discussions over the next few days. He frequently spoke about his daughter, portraying himself as a devoted father committed to providing her with a good life. His stories made me feel closer to him, and my fondness for him grew. He mentioned he was a single father because the mother was not responsible enough to be in the picture. He frequently commented that I would make a great mother, which made me feel good.

After talking for about two weeks, he called me one evening, his voice trembling with emotion. He told me that his mother had just passed away and that he was devastated. He cried hysterically, and my heart ached for him. Having lost my mother, I could empathize with his pain. In his grief, he asked if I could help him fly his aunt from California to attend the funeral. His money was tied up in business transactions, and he needed $1,000 urgently. Without a second thought, I sent him the money to support him in his time of need.

His declarations of love grew more intense after that. He spoke about marrying me and having me move to live with him. He showed me pictures of his beautiful five-bedroom house with an enormous finished basement, a huge chef's kitchen with cherry wood cabinets, and a large bathroom with a jacuzzi tub. He also mentioned me adopting his 14-year-old daughter. He stated that she needed a mother in the house, especially after losing her grandmother. His words were like a balm to my soul. I dreamed of our future together. We decided it was time to meet in person. I flew to see him, filled with anticipation and hope.

He arranged for us to stay in a hotel, which he paid for. They had just held the funeral for his mother, so his house was filled with people. He needed to get away and didn't want to overwhelm me by introducing me to his entire family at once. I was eager to give him a big hug and support him in his time of grieving. When I arrived, I was met by a gentle and loving man. He was on crutches, having injured his knee, and in a lot of pain. Despite his injury, he was attentive and caring, ensuring I was comfortable.

However, there was something peculiar about our meeting. We never left the hotel room. He explained that his injury made getting around difficult, and I accepted his explanation. His lack of eagerness to engage in physical intimacy reinforced my belief in his integrity and respect for me.

While I was with him, he talked a lot about our future and his businesses. He mentioned that my car would be available the following week and that he and his daughter would fly to me so we could sell the vehicle. He said he wanted to marry me in a month, which excited me. He was also eager for me to meet his daughter that day. He stated that she was out of town with her best friend and mother but would be back by 4 p.m. that day. Once 4 p.m. came, he told me there was a delay, and they would return by 8 p.m. By 8 p.m.; he informed me that they wouldn't make it back in time. I found it strange, but I didn't voice my concerns.

The following day, he received a call from his daughter stating that she had lost her grandmother's expensive wedding ring and thought someone had stolen it. She took it without permission because she wanted something from her deceased grandmother. He told me that, unfortunately, he had to drive to the area his daughter was in to figure everything out. He reassured me that he still wanted to marry me in a month and was still flying to me once he received the car to sell. He drove me to the airport and talked to me throughout the day.

After returning home, I continued to communicate with him. I was excited about the car and told him I would share the investment opportunity with my brother and others, which also excited him. He seemed to be in a rush to collect the money and became angry when I told him that my brother and friends were not ready to invest. He turned from this gentle giant to someone cold and thoughtless. This caused me to become very anxious about my investment. I remember crying in the shower and praying that I hadn't just given $2800 to a scammer. He ended up apologizing for his anger and continued talking to me, telling me he loved me, but deep down, I knew I was out $2800.

He remained insistent that he and his daughter would fly to meet me when the car arrived. However, the day before their supposed flight, he called to postpone the delivery. At this point, I knew it was a scam. I demanded my money back and called him a scammer, which provoked him and led to threats. While his threats bothered me, the deception hurt even more. I contacted someone else who knew of him, and they decided to investigate. They discovered that the details he had shared with me were all fabricated.

The funeral home he claimed to own didn't exist. He gave me a fake name and was a career scammer who had gone to jail after scamming people out of almost 1 million dollars. He also lied about his mother dying and being a single father. My heart sank as the reality of the scam became apparent. I realized I had been deceived by a man who had never intended to include me in his life or business. I put myself in a risky situation by visiting a man I barely knew. I felt foolish because my faith in God should have given me the wisdom to make a better decision. I didn't give myself enough time to seek guidance from God due to my overwhelming desperation to have a husband.

The realization that he was a career scammer hit me hard. I felt a deep sense of betrayal and stupidity for having trusted him. The emotional and financial impact of losing $2,800 was overwhelming. I had invested not only my money but also my heart in a relationship that was built on lies.

I thought about reporting the scam to the authorities, but at the time, I wanted him to suffer. Instead, I started waking up at 4 a.m. every morning to pray for his salvation. I did not want this incident to make me bitter because I knew God had much better plans for me. God saw everything he did and would take care of it.

Healing from the emotional wounds took months of waking up at 4 a.m. to pray, write in my journal, and read my Bible. Every time I felt bitterness in my heart, I would pray for his salvation. I also sought support from a therapist, who helped me process my feelings and rebuild my self-esteem. Sharing my experience was therapeutic and reminded me that I was not alone.

Rebuilding trust was a gradual process. I had to learn to trust my judgment and not let the experience define my future relationships. Setting clear boundaries and being more vigilant about potential red flags were crucial steps in regaining my confidence.

I never heard from him again, which was fortunate. This experience taught me valuable lessons about recognizing red flags and being cautious with online relationships. I learned the importance of verifying information and not rushing into financial commitments, no matter how trustworthy someone may seem.

Forgiving myself was crucial to my healing process. I had to understand that I was a victim of a skilled manipulator and not blame myself for being deceived. This self-compassion allowed me to move forward without guilt or regret.

CHAPTER 6

FREEDOM IN OBEDIENCE

For most of my life, I sought fulfillment in my own way, turning away from God and His guidance. I believed happiness lay in following my desires without restraint. I wanted control over my life, free from divine interference. This disobedience led me to some of the darkest and most painful experiences imaginable—attempting suicide, enduring rape, and falling victim to a $2800 scam. Despite God's warnings and the subtle whispers of my conscience, I continued on my destructive path until I couldn't ignore His call any longer.

Since being single, my life has transformed in ways I never imagined. Being single allowed me to reconnect with God and find true healing. I've learned to set healthy boundaries, discern potential partners wisely, and immerse myself in a loving church community. Most importantly, I no longer feel desperate for a relationship; I have found true freedom in God.

The Illusion of Freedom

The world often equates freedom with the ability to do whatever we want, whenever we want. This is the freedom I pursued relentlessly. I chased after relationships, material wealth, and personal achievements, believing these things would bring satisfaction and meaning. However, each pursuit left me emptier than before. My relationships were shallow and often toxic, my material possessions felt hollow, and my achievements were fleeting. The more I sought to fulfill myself, the more I realized I was trapped in a cycle of discontent and despair.

My disobedience to God began with small acts of rebellion—ignoring the quiet nudges of my conscience, disregarding the wisdom of Scripture, and surrounding myself with people who encouraged my self-destructive behaviors. These choices led me into a downward spiral that seemed impossible to escape.

The Turning Point

Despite the pain and suffering, I could feel God reaching out to me. He sent warnings through friends, family, and even strangers. He whispered to me in quiet moments, urging me to turn to Him. But I was stubborn, convinced I could find my own way out of the darkness. It wasn't until I hit rock bottom multiple times that I realized I needed God. My efforts to find fulfillment had led to heartache and regret. I knew I needed to make a change, but I didn't know where to start.

The turning point in my journey came when I finally surrendered to God. I began to pray earnestly, seeking God's guidance and forgiveness. In those moments of vulnerability, I felt His presence more strongly than ever. He wrapped me in His love and grace, reassuring me I was not alone and that there was hope for a better future.

Redefining Freedom

Singleness became the unexpected catalyst for my transformation. In the solitude of being single, I found the space to reconnect with God and begin my healing journey. Without the distractions of a relationship, I focused on my spiritual growth and listened to God's voice more clearly. During this period, I discovered the true meaning of freedom—not in doing whatever I wanted, but in surrendering my will to God and trusting Him completely.

Freedom in the Christian faith isn't merely the absence of restrictions or the ability to do as we please. It's a profound liberation from sin and the empowerment to live according to God's will. This freedom brings peace and fulfillment that the world cannot offer. By obeying God, we align ourselves with His perfect plan for our lives, which is far greater than anything we could ever imagine.

Through obedience to God, I learned to set healthy boundaries in my life. I began to understand my worth as a child of God and refused to settle for anything less than what He had planned for me. I discerned potential partners more wisely, no longer driven by desperation but by a desire to align my life with God's will. I also found solace and support in a loving church community, where I was encouraged and uplifted in my walk with Christ.

Most importantly, I no longer felt desperate for a relationship. The emptiness I once tried to fill with earthly things was now filled with God's love and grace. I realized that true freedom comes from obeying God—following His commandments, seeking His guidance, and trusting in His plans. This freedom brought a peace that surpassed all understanding, a joy that was not dependent on my circumstances, and a purpose rooted in something far greater than myself.

Living in True Freedom

True freedom begins with surrender. Surrendering our will to God and acknowledging that His ways are higher than ours is not an easy process; it requires humility, trust, and a willingness to let go of our own desires. But as we surrender to God, we begin to experience the fullness of life that He promises.

One of the first steps I took towards true freedom was immersing myself in God's Word. The Bible became my guide and source of strength. Through Scripture, I learned about God's character, His promises, and His plans for my life. I discovered that God's commandments are not burdensome rules meant to restrict me but loving instructions designed to protect me and lead me to a life of abundance.

Prayer also became an essential part of my journey. It was through prayer that I developed a deeper relationship with God. I poured my heart into Him, sharing my fears, hopes, and struggles. In return, He comforted, guided, and filled me with His peace. Prayer became a lifeline, connecting me to the One who knows me better than I know myself.

Healing and Restoration

One of the most profound aspects of my journey towards freedom was the healing and restoration that God brought into my life. The scars from my past were deep, and I carried a lot of pain and shame. But as I surrendered my brokenness to God, He began to heal me in ways I never thought possible.

God's healing was not just emotional but also spiritual and relational. He restored my sense of worth and identity, reminding me that I am His beloved child. He healed my relationships, helping me to forgive those who had hurt me and to seek reconciliation where possible. He also healed my mind, freeing me from the lies and harmful patterns of thinking that had kept me in bondage.

This healing process was not instantaneous; it took time and required patience and perseverance. But with each step of obedience, I experienced more of God's grace and love. He walked with me through my pain, comforting me and giving me the strength to keep moving forward.

The Power of Obedience

Obedience to God is not always easy, but it is always rewarding. It requires faith and trust, especially when we don't understand His ways or when His instructions seem difficult. But as we obey Him, we experience the power of His presence in our lives.

Through obedience, I learned to relinquish my need for control and trust in God's sovereignty. I discovered His plans are far better than anything I could plan for myself. Obedience also taught me to rely on God's strength rather than my own. When I felt weak and overwhelmed, His grace sustained me and gave me the power to persevere.

Obedience to God also brings blessings that we cannot obtain through our own efforts. As I obeyed God, I experienced His provision and favor in ways that amazed me. He opened doors that I never thought possible and miraculously provided for my needs. His blessings were not always material but were always abundant and life-giving.

Living in True Freedom

Living in true freedom means living in the fullness of God's love and grace. It means being free from the bondage of sin and the enemy's lies. It means walking in the truth of who we are in Christ and embracing the life He has called us to live.

This freedom is not just for our own benefit but for the glory of God and the good of others. As we obey God, our lives testify to His faithfulness and love. We become a light in the darkness, pointing others to the hope and freedom we have found in Christ.

Living in true freedom also means embracing our identity and purpose in Christ. Our past mistakes or our current struggles no longer define us. We are defined by who we are in Him—beloved children of God, chosen and called for a purpose. This purpose is not just for our own fulfillment but for advancing God's kingdom and sharing His love with the world.

The Journey Continues

My journey towards freedom through obedience to God is far from over. It is a daily walk of faith, trust, and surrender. There are still challenges and struggles, but there is also a deep and abiding peace that comes from knowing that I am walking in God's will.

Each day, I am reminded of God's faithfulness and unfailing love. I am reminded that true freedom is found not in living for myself but for Him.

As I continue this journey, I pray that my life will testify to God's grace and power. I hope others will see the freedom and healing He has brought into my life and be drawn to Him. For it is in Him that we find true freedom, and through obedience to Him, we experience the fullness of life that He has promised.

The Foundation of Obedience

The foundation of obedience is trust. Trusting God means believing He is good, His plans for us are for our benefit, and His commandments are given out of love. This trust is built through a relationship with Him, nurtured by prayer, studying the Bible, and experiencing His faithfulness in our lives. As we know God more intimately, our trust in Him grows, making it easier to surrender and obey.

The Role of the Holy Spirit

One of the most powerful aspects of our journey towards obedience and freedom is the role of the Holy Spirit. When we accept Jesus as our Savior, the Holy Spirit dwells within us, guiding us, convicting us of sin, and empowering us to live a life that pleases God. The Holy Spirit gives us the strength to resist temptation, the wisdom to make godly decisions, and the courage to step out in faith.

Through the Holy Spirit, we experience God's presence in our daily lives. He comforts us in times of sorrow, encourages us when we feel weak, and fills us with joy and peace. The more we yield to the Holy Spirit, the more we are transformed into the likeness of Christ, and the more we walk in the freedom that obedience to God brings.

Overcoming Challenges

Obedience to God does not mean that we will never face challenges or difficulties. There will be times when obedience requires great sacrifice and perseverance. However, these challenges are opportunities for growth and a deeper dependence on God. Each trial we face invites us to trust God more fully and rely on His strength rather than our own.

In my journey, there were moments when obedience felt like an uphill battle. Sometimes, I was tempted to return to my old ways of seeking fulfillment. But in those moments, I clung to God's promises and reminded myself of the freedom I had found in Him. I learned to take my struggles to Him in prayer and to immerse myself in His Word. Through these practices, I found the strength to continue on the path of obedience.

The Fruit of Obedience

One of the most beautiful aspects of obedience is the fruit it produces in our lives. As we align ourselves with God's will, we begin to see the evidence of His work in us. The Bible describes this fruit as love, joy, peace, patience, kindness, goodness, faithfulness, gentleness, and self-control (Galatians 5:22-23). These qualities are a testament to the transformative power of God's Spirit within us.

In my own life, I began to see this fruit in various ways. My relationships improved as I learned to love others with the love of Christ. I experienced a deep and abiding joy that was not dependent on my circumstances. I found peace amid chaos, patience in times of waiting, and kindness even towards those who had hurt me. These changes were not my efforts but God's work in me as I yielded to Him.

Freedom in Community

Freedom through obedience is not something we experience in isolation. It is meant to be lived out in the context of community. The church is a vital part of our journey towards freedom, providing support, accountability, and encouragement. In community, we find people who share our faith, pray for us, walk with us through difficult times, and celebrate with us in moments of victory.

Being part of a loving church community has been a significant part of my healing and growth. In this community, I found people who accepted me as I was, who believed in God's work in my life, and who encouraged me to keep moving forward. Together, we studied God's Word, worshipped, and served others. This fellowship strengthened my faith and deepened my understanding of what it means to live in true freedom.

The Impact of Our Freedom

The freedom we experience through obedience to God is not just for our benefit. It is meant to have a ripple effect, impacting those around us and extending the kingdom of God. As we live in the freedom of Christ, our lives become a testimony of His love and power. Others see the transformation in us and are drawn to the hope we have found.

Our obedience can inspire others to seek God and trust His goodness. It can open doors for conversations about faith and provide opportunities to share the gospel. Our lives, marked by freedom and joy, can be a powerful witness to the world of what it means to follow Jesus.

A Life of Purpose

Living in true freedom means living a life of purpose. It means recognizing that we are part of God's larger plan and that our lives have significance beyond our own personal desires. As we obey God, we discover His unique calling for each of us and how we can contribute to His work in the world.

For me, this has meant using my experiences and my journey towards freedom to help others who are struggling. It has meant sharing my story, offering support and encouragement, and pointing others to the hope and healing I have found in Christ. It has meant being available for God to use me in whatever way He sees fit, trusting that His plans are good.

Conclusion

Obedience to God is the key to true freedom. It is through surrendering our wills to Him and aligning our lives with His purposes that we experience the profound liberation from sin and the empowerment to live according to His will. This journey of obedience is not without its challenges, but it is filled with the promise of transformation, healing, and abundant life.

As we walk in obedience, we find the freedom to be who God created us to be. We experience the fullness of His love and grace, the joy of His presence, and the peace that surpasses all understanding. We are no longer bound by the lies of the enemy or the weight of our past. We are free to live in the light of His truth and to embrace the life He has called us to live.

My journey toward freedom through obedience to God has been one of my life's most challenging and rewarding experiences. It has required faith, trust, and a willingness to let go of my own desires. But it has also brought me peace, joy, and fulfillment. It has shown me that true freedom is not found in living for myself but in living for Him.

1. Reflect on Your Transformation:

How has being single allowed you to reconnect with God and find healing in your life? Describe specific moments or changes that illustrate this transformation.

2. Understanding True Freedom:

What does true freedom mean to you now compared to when you sought fulfillment on your own terms? How has your understanding of freedom evolved through your journey with God?

3. Identifying Turning Points:

Can you pinpoint a specific moment or experience that served as a turning point in your journey back to God? What made this moment significant, and how did it impact your faith and actions?

4. Healing from Past Pain:

How has God helped you heal from the darkest experiences in your past. What steps did you take to surrender these pains to God, and what healing did you experience as a result?

5. Living in Obedience:

In what ways has living in obedience to God brought peace, joy, and purpose to your life? Reflect on specific instances where following God's will has led to unexpected blessings or personal growth.

CHAPTER 7

FROM LUKEWARM TO ON FIRE: A JOURNEY OF FAITH

For a significant period, I regarded myself as a Christian. However, I must confess that I was living a lukewarm life-style. Even though I believed in God, I never really put in the effort to practice my faith. I would attend church sporadically, maybe once or twice a year, but it never felt like a priority. My social life revolved around attending clubs and parties rather than engaging in God-approved activities. As a result, I never felt a strong connection with God, and my faith never took root in my heart. I didn't realize it then, but I was living a life full of sin with no repentance. Looking back, I can see that I was lost and searching for something, but I didn't know what.

The term "lukewarm Christian" comes from a passage in the Bible, specifically Revelation 3:15–16, where Jesus addresses the church in Laodicea: "I know all the things you do, that you are neither hot nor cold. I wish that you were one or the other! But since you are like lukewarm water, neither hot nor cold, I will spit you out of my mouth!"

This stark imagery captures the seriousness of being spiritually tepid. A lukewarm Christian is someone who professes faith in Christ but whose life shows little evidence of genuine commitment, passion, or transformation.

Characteristics of a Lukewarm Christian

Lukewarm Christians often exhibit inconsistency in spiritual disciplines such as prayer, Bible reading, and worship. These activities may be performed out of obligation rather than genuine desire. Church attendance might be sporadic, and engagement in community or service activities is minimal.

They might read the Bible occasionally but not deeply engage with its teachings or apply them to daily life. Prayers may be routine and hurried, lacking heartfelt communication with God. This inconsistency reflects a more profound disconnect between professed beliefs and daily living.

Compartmentalized Faith

Another hallmark of lukewarm Christianity is compartmentalization. Faith is confined to specific areas of life, such as Sunday mornings or certain social circles, while other aspects of life remain unaffected by one's beliefs. This separation leads to a dual existence where Christian principles are not integrated into everyday decisions, behaviors, and interactions.

A lukewarm Christian might act differently at work, home, and church, adopting varying sets of values and behaviors depending on the context. This lack of integration prevents the transformative power of faith from fully influencing one's life and undermines the witness to others.

Lack of Passion and Zeal

Passion and zeal are often missing in the life of a lukewarm Christian. There is a noticeable absence of enthusiasm for sharing the gospel, participating in mission work, or engaging in activities that promote spiritual growth. This lack of enthusiasm can lead to spiritual stagnation and a sense of complacency.

For instance, a lukewarm Christian might avoid discussions about faith, evangelism, or more profound theological questions, preferring to focus on comfortable, non-confrontational aspects of religion. This reluctance stems from a fear of discomfort, conflict, or the demands that a more passionate faith might entail.

Worldly Priorities

A significant indicator of lukewarmness is prioritizing worldly pursuits over spiritual ones. Material wealth, social status, career advancement, and personal comfort often take precedence over seeking God's kingdom and righteousness. This misalignment of priorities can lead to compromised values and ethical decisions.

For example, a lukewarm Christian might spend significant time and resources on personal hobbies, entertainment, or material possessions while neglecting opportunities for service, generosity, or spiritual growth. This focus on the temporal rather than the eternal reflects a skewed understanding of what it means to follow Christ.

Causes of Lukewarm Christianity

Cultural Influence

One of the primary causes of lukewarm Christianity is the pervasive influence of secular culture. Maintaining a vibrant and countercultural faith can be challenging in a society that often values materialism, individualism, and relativism. The constant bombardment of secular values through media, education, and social norms can erode spiritual fervor.

The cultural emphasis on success and self-fulfillment can lead Christians to prioritize personal goals over spiritual ones. The relativistic view that all beliefs are equally valid can dilute the distinctiveness and urgency of the Christian message, making it easy to adopt a more passive and complacent approach to faith.

Complacency and Comfort

Complacency and comfort are significant contributors to lukewarmness. When life is relatively easy and free from persecution or significant hardship, settling into a routine requiring minimal spiritual effort is tempting. This comfort can lead to a false sense of security and self-sufficiency.

In a prosperous society, a Christian may not feel the need to rely on God daily or seek deeper spiritual growth. The absence of pressing challenges or crises can lead to a shallow faith that is content with the status quo rather than striving for greater intimacy with God and impact in the world.

Lack of Discipleship and Accountability

The absence of solid discipleship and accountability structures within the church can also contribute to lukewarmness. Without regular teaching, mentorship, and community support, it is easy for believers to drift into spiritual apathy. Discipleship provides the necessary guidance and encouragement to pursue a vibrant faith.

A church focusing more on prosperity and abundance than building personal relationships through discipleship may unintentionally create an environment where individual spiritual development is overlooked. Without accountability, Christians may lack the encouragement and assistance necessary to work on areas of spiritual struggle and strive for greater maturity.

Spiritual Warfare

Lukewarmness can also be attributed to spiritual warfare. The enemy seeks to undermine the faith of believers by fostering doubt, distraction, and discouragement. Spiritual attacks can manifest subtly, leading to a gradual decline in spiritual vitality.

If a Christian experiences persistent doubts about God's goodness or the truth of scripture, it can erode their faith and lead to a passive and disengaged spiritual life if left unaddressed. Recognizing and addressing this spiritual battle is crucial to overcoming lukewarmness.

The Consequences of Lukewarm Christianity

Ineffective Witness

One of the most significant consequences of lukewarm Christianity is an ineffective witness. When Christians fail to live out their faith authentically and passionately, it undermines their ability to influence others positively. A lukewarm faith does not inspire curiosity or admiration but may lead to skepticism and disinterest.

Non-believers who observe the life of a lukewarm Christian may not see much of a difference between their behavior and that of the secular world. This lack of distinctiveness can hinder opportunities for evangelism and discipleship, as the persuasive power of a transformed life is missing.

Spiritual Stagnation

Lukewarmness leads to spiritual stagnation, where growth and maturity are hindered. Without a deep and active engagement with God, believers miss out on the fullness of life that Jesus promises. This stagnation can lead to a sense of unfulfillment and frustration.

A lukewarm Christian might find themselves going through the motions of faith without experiencing the joy, peace, and purpose of a rich relationship with God. This stagnation prevents them from reaching their full potential and experiencing the abundant life Jesus offers.

Compromised Values

When faith is lukewarm, it becomes easier to compromise on values and ethical decisions. Without a firm foundation and a passionate commitment to God's principles, believers may succumb to societal pressures and make choices that are inconsistent with their professed beliefs.

For instance, a lukewarm Christian might engage in dishonest business practices, participate in gossip, or tolerate immoral behavior. These compromises damage their witness and hinder their spiritual growth and integrity.

Missed Opportunities

Lukewarm Christians miss out on opportunities to impact the world for Christ. They are less likely to engage in service, evangelism, and mission work without a vigorous and active faith. These missed opportunities result in a diminished influence and a failure to fulfill God's calling.

A lukewarm Christian may overlook opportunities to serve the poor, share the gospel, or mentor younger believers, missing chances to make a meaningful impact and fulfill the Great Commission.

Rekindling a Fervent Faith

Self-Examination and Repentance

The journey from lukewarmness to genuine faith begins with self-examination and repentance. Recognizing areas of spiritual complacency and confessing them to God is the first step toward renewal. This process involves assessing one's spiritual practices, priorities, and motivations honestly.

Taking time to reflect on one's spiritual life through prayer and journaling can reveal areas of neglect and inconsistency. Repentance involves turning away from these patterns and committing to a renewed focus on God and His purposes.

Recommitment to Spiritual Disciplines

Rekindling a fervent faith requires a recommitment to spiritual disciplines such as prayer, Bible study, worship, and fellowship. These practices are essential for cultivating a deep and abiding relationship with God.

Setting aside dedicated time each day for prayer and Scripture reading can help reignite passion and intimacy with God. Joining a small group or Bible study can provide accountability and support, encouraging growth and commitment.

Pursuing Holistic Discipleship

Holistic discipleship involves integrating faith into every aspect of life, breaking down the compartments that separate the sacred from the secular. This integration requires a conscious effort to live out Christian values in all areas of life, including work, relationships, and leisure.

A Christian might seek to apply biblical principles to their career, treating colleagues with respect, pursuing excellence, and making ethical decisions. This holistic approach ensures that faith is not confined to specific areas but permeates every aspect of life.

Engaging in Service and Mission

Actively engaging in service and mission work can reignite a passion for God's kingdom. Serving others and participating in evangelism provide tangible expressions of faith and opportunities to witness God's power and love in action.

Volunteering at a local shelter, participating in a mission trip, or supporting community outreach programs can deepen one's faith and commitment. These experiences impact others and transform the believer's heart and perspective.

Seeking Accountability and Mentorship

Accountability and mentorship are crucial for maintaining spiritual fervor. It's essential to have trusted individuals who can provide guidance, support, and encouragement to ensure that one's faith remains vibrant and active. These relationships offer honest reflection, constructive feedback, and spiritual growth opportunities.

For instance, seeking a mentor within the church—someone more spiritually mature and experienced—can offer valuable insights and wisdom. This mentor can provide practical advice on overcoming spiritual challenges, maintaining a commitment to spiritual disciplines, and integrating faith into daily life.

Being part of an accountability group creates a supportive environment where members can share their struggles, victories, and goals. Regular check-ins and mutual encouragement foster a sense of community and shared purpose, making it easier to maintain a strong faith.

The Story of Peter

Peter famously denied knowing Jesus three times during a moment of fear and uncertainty. Despite this act of denial, Peter's journey did not end there. His faith, though faltering, was not extinguished.

After witnessing the resurrection of Jesus, Peter experienced a profound transformation. Filled with the Holy Spirit, he became a bold and unwavering leader of the early church. His initial failure became a pivotal moment in his spiritual growth, demonstrating that even in weakness, one's faith can be renewed and strengthened.

Peter's story is a testament to the power of redemption and the possibility of profound growth in one's faith journey.

Conclusion

Being a lukewarm Christian is a condition that many believers struggle with at some point in their spiritual journey. It is characterized by inconsistency, compartmentalization, lack of passion, and misplaced priorities. The causes of lukewarmness are varied, including cultural influences, complacency, a lack of discipleship, and spiritual warfare. The consequences are significant, leading to an ineffective witness, spiritual stagnation, compromised values, and missed opportunities.

Rekindling a fervent faith is possible through self-examination, repentance, recommitment to spiritual disciplines, holistic discipleship, service, and seeking accountability and mentorship. Both biblical and modern stories of transformation illustrate the power of God to renew and ignite a passionate faith. The church plays a crucial role in supporting believers by creating a nurturing environment, encouraging authentic worship, and fostering community and service.

Maintaining a strong faith ultimately requires daily commitment to spiritual practices, active participation in a supportive community, striving for holiness, and engaging in mission. By taking these steps, believers can transition from lukewarmness to a vibrant, impactful faith that honors God and transforms lives.

JOURNAL ENTRY

1. Self-Examination:

What specific areas of my life have I been lukewarm in my faith? How have I compartmentalized my faith, and what are the consequences I have experienced because of this?

2. Repentance and Renewal:

What steps can I take to repent from my lukewarmness and seek genuine transformation? What spiritual disciplines (prayer, Bible study, worship) can I recommit to in order to strengthen my relationship with God?

3. Holistic Discipleship:

How can I integrate my faith into every aspect of my life, including my work, relationships, and leisure activities? What practical changes can I make to ensure that my faith influences my daily decisions and interactions?

4. Service and Mission:

In what ways can I actively engage in service and mission work to reignite my passion for God's kingdom? What specific opportunities for service and evangelism can I pursue to make a meaningful impact in my community and beyond?

5. Accountability and Mentorship:

Who can I seek out for accountability and mentorship to support my spiritual growth? How can I build or strengthen relationships with individuals or groups within my church community to foster mutual encouragement and spiritual development?

CHAPTER 8

BECOMING A PROVERBS 31 WOMAN: A JOURNEY OF TRANSFORMATION

When people describe a woman as godly, they often refer to the qualities attributed to the Proverbs 31 woman in the Bible. However, in today's society, it can be challenging to understand the meaning behind those characteristics. With the rise of feminism and the push towards being an independent woman, many women are taught that they do not need a man or anyone else. We are often told that it is okay to be promiscuous and dress immodestly. Therefore, it can be challenging to determine what it means to be a godly woman in modern times. As a result, when we hear that we should be hardworking, selfless, family-oriented, capable of managing a household, caring for children, and maintaining our faith, we may perceive it as foreign and degrading.

In the past, I was completely unaware of the qualities that define a Proverbs 31 woman. My behavior was far from being considered virtuous. I had a habit of using foul language, enjoyed going out to clubs, and often indulged in excessive drinking. I was constantly in search of male attention, and I would go to any lengths to get it, be it through manipulation or by engaging in promiscuous behavior. The validation I received from men was something that I craved, and I wasn't willing to let go of it. This led to a cycle of seeking attention, feeling validated, and seeking more attention. I was utterly oblivious to the fact that I was hurting myself and those around me and that my actions were not reflective of the values that I wanted to uphold in my life.

Before I decided to give my life to Christ in 2021, I had a tumultuous past of jumping from one relationship to another without any intention of getting married or pleasing God. I was not a committed Christian during those times, and I spent little to no time reading the Bible. Even after getting married, I failed to be the helpmate that a godly man desires. My behavior had a lot to do with my lukewarm attitude towards Christianity.

However, after I surrendered my life to Christ, He revealed the true meaning of being a virtuous woman in His eyes. Despite this, my past mistakes continued to haunt me, and I struggled with feelings of condemnation. I felt like I could never be the ideal woman that God intended me to be, especially given my track record. Nevertheless, I remained steadfast in my faith, trusting Him to transform me into the godly woman He created me to be.

The passage in Proverbs 31 is considered a standard for the ideal woman. It describes the positive attributes and qualities that people may seek in a woman. However, it's important to remember that we are all imperfect beings, and it's natural to have areas in our lives that need improvement. When we seek God's healing in our lives, it's not always an instant process. It can be uncomfortable and even painful at times. But during this journey, it's important to remain rooted in God and trust that we are in the safest place possible. It's through this trust and reliance on God that we can experience true healing and growth.

The Bible teaches us in Psalm 139:14 that we are fearfully and wonderfully made by God. This means that each one of us is a unique and precious creation with our own set of talents, abilities, and callings. When we surrender our lives to Jesus Christ, we are forgiven of our sins and become part of God's family. As His adopted children, we are loved and valued beyond measure, and we have a vital role in His kingdom.

As children of God, we can receive His grace and unconditional love. This love has the power to transform our lives in remarkable ways, heal our deepest wounds, calm our fears, and guide us toward a brighter future. God's love is all-encompassing, life-giving, and eternal, and it can help us overcome any obstacle in life.

As mentioned, the journey of spiritual growth is not always easy. It requires us to live a life of faith, humility, and surrender. It involves cultivating virtues such as patience, kindness, forgiveness, and generosity, which help us become more like Christ and reflect His love and light to the world.

Thankfully, Jesus offers comfort during this journey. In Matthew 11:28–30, He invites us to come to Him when we are weary and carry heavy burdens, and He promises to give us rest. When we take His yoke upon ourselves and learn from Him, we can find rest for our souls. Jesus is gentle and humble in heart, and His yoke is easy, and His burden is light.

This means that even during difficult times, we can take comfort in knowing that God is always with us, supporting and guiding us towards the best possible outcomes.

It is through these trials that we learn to lean on Him more fully and rely on His guidance and wisdom. As we grow in our relationship with Him, we begin to see the world and ourselves through His eyes, gaining a deeper understanding of our purpose and calling in life. This understanding empowers us to live our lives with greater passion and intention. An important thing to remember regarding personal growth is that it doesn't happen in isolation. To truly grow and develop, we need to surround ourselves with a support system of individuals who share our beliefs and values and who can offer us the support, encouragement, and accountability that we need to keep pushing ourselves to be our best selves.

Whether working towards a specific goal or simply trying to develop individually, having a support system is critical. These individuals can offer us a sounding board for our ideas, a source of inspiration and motivation, and a sense of accountability that can keep us on track when we're feeling discouraged or overwhelmed.

Of course, finding your tribe isn't always easy. It takes time, effort, and a willingness to be vulnerable and open with others. But the rewards can be immeasurable, both in personal growth and in the relationships and connections we develop along the way. When we become disheartened, they can remind us of the promises made by God and assist us in remaining committed to fulfilling our goals.

On this journey, you may also believe that the Proverbs 31 woman can only be emulated by married women with children. However, this is a common misconception that is far from the truth. In reality, the qualities that the Proverbs 31 woman embodies, such as wisdom, hard work, kindness, and generosity, are not exclusive to married women with children. They can be cultivated and demonstrated by women in any season of life, including single women.

In fact, the single season of your life can be the most critical time to cultivate these qualities. Being single can allow you to focus on personal growth and development without the added responsibilities of marriage and children. This can be a time to discover your passions, develop your skills, and build your character. By doing so, you can become a woman of influence, impact, and purpose. It is during this time that you can cultivate a deep and intimate relationship with God and discover the unique purpose for which He created you.

Embarking on a journey of self-improvement is a continuous process that demands unwavering commitment and dedication to develop and progress. It's crucial to understand that becoming a better version of oneself is not a one-time event but a lifelong pursuit. The process of self-improvement involves taking small, deliberate, and consistent steps toward enhancing oneself, which requires a willingness to learn, adapt, and grow. This journey requires obeying God, praying, allowing God to point out anything that offends Him, and setting realistic goals.

By developing your relationship with God and discovering your true identity in Christ, you can save yourself from heartache and disappointment in future relationships and decisions. You can make wise choices and avoid relationships with men and opportunities not meant for you. Ultimately, by investing in yourself during your single season, you increase your chances of building a successful and fulfilling life that is aligned with God's plan.

A Proverbs 31 woman is characterized by being compassionate, wise, trustworthy, virtuous, faithful, diligent, kind, hardworking, loving, and more precious than jewels. However, we must remember that possessing these qualities is a lifelong pursuit. We are not perfect, but as long as we pursue and keep our eyes on God, He will continuously shape us into the woman He created us to be.

JOURNAL ENTRY

1. Reflect on Your Journey:

Consider your past behaviors and lifestyle. How has your understanding of what it means to be a godly woman changed over time? What specific events or realizations led to these changes?

2. Identifying Qualities:

Look at the attributes of the Proverbs 31 woman. Which qualities do you feel you already embody, and which do you think you need to work on? How can you start to cultivate these qualities in your daily life?

3. Overcoming Condemnation:

Reflect on the feelings of condemnation you've experienced due to past mistakes. How have you been able to find peace and forgiveness through your faith? What practices or scriptures have helped you the most in this area?

4. Community and Support:

Think about the importance of having a support system in your journey of spiritual growth. Who are the key people in your life that support your faith and growth? How can you nurture these relationships further?

5. Embracing Singleness:

Consider the advantages of being single in your pursuit of becoming a Proverbs 31 woman. How can you use this time to focus on personal growth and deepening your relationship with God? What specific goals or activities can help you make the most of this season of life?

CHAPTER 9

FAITHFUL PURSUIT: NAVIGATING CHRISTIAN DATING WITH NON-NEGOTIABLES

Navigating the world of Christian dating can be a daunting task, especially if you have a history of past relationships that didn't work out. As a woman of faith, you desire to be pursued by a man with similar values and beliefs. However, the process of finding the right partner can feel overwhelming and confusing at times. It's essential to take time to reflect on your values and priorities and to seek guidance from trusted friends and mentors. Remember that God has a plan for your life, including your romantic relationships. Don't be afraid to take things slow, and be intentional in your pursuit of a partner who shares your faith and values. However, it's important to remember that just because someone is pursuing you doesn't necessarily mean they are God-sent.

Developing a solid relationship with God can be a transformative experience that helps you realize your true worth and gain sharper discernment. As you deepen your connection, you may find that you can more easily identify and eliminate any men who are simply there to distract you from your purpose.

It's important to remember that the enemy will often send counterfeits to try to derail you from your path. That's why setting boundaries and establishing non-negotiables before putting yourself out there is crucial. By taking the time to identify what you will and won't tolerate in a relationship, you can avoid wasting time on people who don't align with your values and goals.

So, what are some non-negotiables that every godly woman should have? Here are four that you might consider:

1. He must love Jesus and grow in Him daily.

To be a good leader, a man must first be led by Christ. This means that he is guided by the principles and teachings of the Bible and seeks to live a life that reflects those values. Deuteronomy 6:5 emphasizes the importance of loving God with all our heart, soul, and strength, and this is a fundamental principle for any man who wishes to lead a family.

However, it's not enough for a man to say he loves Jesus. His actions, behavior, and words must also reflect his faith and his commitment to Christ. You should look for someone whose actions mirror Christ-like qualities, such as love, compassion, and forgiveness. A man who embodies these qualities is more likely to be a good partner and leader and to create a strong foundation for a lasting relationship.

In the journey of finding a godly partner, observing his daily walk with Christ is essential. Does he dedicate time each day to prayer and studying the Bible? Is he active in his church community, participating in worship, service, and fellowship? His commitment to growing in faith should be evident in his daily life, not just in his words.

A man who loves Jesus will also seek to lead by example, showing kindness, humility, and a servant's heart in all areas of his life. He should be someone who encourages your own spiritual growth and walks alongside you on your faith journey. Together, you can build a relationship centered on Christ, which is the strongest foundation for a lasting and fulfilling partnership.

2. He must be willing to wait until marriage to have sex.

A lustful man will have no desire to wait until marriage to have sex. He will take every opportunity to lure you into the bedroom and then guilt-trip you if you decline. A godly man will spiritually lead you towards God and prioritize protecting your soul. 1 Corinthians 6:18 says, "Run from sexual sin! No other sin so clearly affects the body as this one does. For sexual immorality is a sin against your own body."

Waiting until marriage to have sex is a significant commitment and a test of character and self-control. It demonstrates a man's respect for God's commandments and his respect for you as a person. A man who is willing to wait understands the value of purity and the importance of building a relationship based on more than just physical attraction.

In today's society, where casual relationships and instant gratification are often celebrated, a man who chooses to wait until marriage stands out as someone with strong convictions and integrity. He recognizes that true love is patient and that the physical aspect of a relationship is just one part of a deeper, more meaningful connection.

A godly man will also understand the importance of setting boundaries to protect your purity and honor your commitment to God. He will support you in your decision to wait and encourage you to stay strong in your convictions. This mutual respect and support can strengthen your relationship and build trust, which is essential for a successful marriage.

3. He must not love the world.

When trying to get to know someone, it's essential to pay attention to their taste in music, favorite hangouts, behaviors, and mindset. These things can give you a good idea of who they are and how they approach life.

In addition, it's also important to consider a person's values and beliefs. 1 John 2:15 cautions against loving the world and its offerings above God. While no one is perfect, a man who loves God will have a desire to please Him and live according to His will. This can manifest in many different ways, such as how they treat others, how they spend their time and resources, and what they prioritize in life.

A man who does not love the world will demonstrate this through his actions and choices. He will prioritize his relationship with God over material possessions, social status, and worldly pleasures. His focus will be on eternal values rather than temporary gains, and he will seek to live a life that honors God in every aspect.

This perspective is crucial to building a strong and lasting relationship. A man who loves God more than the world will encourage you to grow in your faith and will support you in your spiritual journey. He will understand the importance of living a life that reflects God's love and will strive to be a positive influence in your life.

Furthermore, a man who does not love the world will be less likely to be swayed by external pressures and temptations. He will have a firm foundation in his faith, which will help him navigate the challenges and trials that come with life and relationships. Stability and steadfastness are essential qualities for a partner who will support you through thick and thin.

4. He must have the desire to get married.

When it comes to dating, a man devoted to God has a different approach than most. He understands that dating should never be taken lightly and is a serious step towards commitment and marriage. For this reason, he will only consider dating when he is truly ready for marriage, and he won't waste your time if he doesn't see himself marrying you in the future.

In the eyes of God, marriage is a significant commitment that should not be taken lightly. The Bible teaches us that marriage should always be the goal, and it is not about having long-term girlfriends or boyfriends. Genesis 2:24 says, "This explains why a man leaves his father and mother and is joined to his wife, and the two are united into one." Therefore, the primary objective of all Christians who are seeking a partner should be to have a Kingdom marriage that is based on mutual love, respect, and commitment.

A true man of God has an unshakeable desire to bring glory to the Almighty. He knows that he is not perfect, but he remains steadfast in his pursuit of spiritual growth every day. His actions bear witness to his unwavering commitment to God, and he strives to live a life that is pleasing to Him. That's why he takes dating and relationships seriously and approaches them with the same level of commitment and devotion toward his faith.

A man who is serious about marriage will also be intentional in his actions and words. He will make his intentions clear from the beginning and will take steps to build a relationship that leads to marriage. This means being honest, transparent, and committed to working through any challenges that arise.

In addition, a man who desires to get married will prioritize building a strong foundation for your relationship. He will invest time and effort in getting to know you, understanding your values and beliefs, and building trust. He will also seek guidance from God and wise counsel from trusted mentors and friends to ensure that your relationship is built on solid ground.

It's also important to note that a man who is ready for marriage will be willing to make sacrifices and compromises for the sake of the relationship. He will understand that marriage requires effort, patience, and a willingness to put the needs of your partner above your own. Selflessness and commitment are essential for building a lasting and fulfilling marriage.

Practical Steps for Establishing Non-Negotiables

Establishing non-negotiables is an essential part of preparing for a godly relationship. Here are some practical steps to help you identify and stick to your non-negotiables:

1. Seek guidance from God:

Pray and seek guidance from God as you establish your non-negotiables. Ask Him to give you wisdom and discernment in identifying what is truly important in a relationship and to help you stay true to your values.

Regular prayer and meditation on God's word can help you maintain focus and clarity on what you desire in a partner. This spiritual practice can also provide you with the strength to uphold your standards, even when faced with challenging situations or temptations. Consistent communication with God can reinforce your commitment to your non-negotiables and ensure that your choices align with your faith and values.

2. Reflect on Your Values and Beliefs:

Take time to reflect on your core values and beliefs. What is most important to you in a relationship? What are your deal-breakers? Write down your non-negotiables and refer to them regularly to remind yourself of what you are looking for in a partner.

3. Consult trusted friends and mentors:

Seek advice from trusted friends and mentors who share your faith and values. They can provide valuable insights and support as you navigate the dating process and help you stay accountable for your non-negotiables. Their perspectives can offer a different viewpoint and help you recognize any blind spots you might have. Additionally, sharing your journey with others can create a support system that encourages and strengthens you in your decisions, ensuring you stay true to your principles and avoid compromising on what truly matters to you in a relationship.

In conclusion, navigating the world of Christian dating can be challenging, but by establishing non-negotiables and seeking a partner who shares your faith and values, you can build a strong foundation for a lasting and fulfilling relationship. Remember to prioritize your relationship with God, set boundaries, and be intentional in your pursuit of a godly partner. With patience, discernment, and trust in God's plan, you can find a partner who will support you in your faith journey and help you build a kingdom marriage that honors God.

1. Reflecting on My Values and Beliefs:

What are my core values and beliefs that I hold dear in a relationship?

How do these values influence my decisions and actions in my dating life?

In what ways do I see these values aligning with God's teachings?

2. Identifying My Non-Negotiables:

What are the key non-negotiables I need in a partner to ensure a godly relationship?

How have past relationships helped me understand what I will and won't tolerate?

How can I clearly communicate these non-negotiables to potential partners?

3. Seeking Guidance and Discernment:

How can I involve God more deeply in my process of finding a partner?

Who are the trusted friends and mentors I can turn to for advice and accountability in my dating journey?

How can regular prayer and meditation on God's word strengthen my resolve to uphold my standards?

4. Observing Christ-Like Qualities in a Partner:

What specific actions, behaviors, and words reflect a genuine commitment to Christ in a potential partner?

How can I discern if someone is truly led by Christ and not just claiming to be?

What qualities should I look for that indicate a man's dedication to growing in his faith daily?

5. Patience and Intentionality in Pursuing a Godly Partner:

How can I balance taking things slow with being intentional in my pursuit of a godly partner?

What steps can I take to ensure I am not settling for a counterfeit relationship sent to distract me from my purpose?

How can I stay focused on God's plan for my life, trusting that He has a purpose for my romantic relationships?

CHAPTER 10

GUARDING THE HEART: EMBRACING GODLY BOUNDARIES

As someone who has struggled with being a people-pleaser and workaholic, I know firsthand what it's like to have your boundaries violated.

In my personal experience, I have found it particularly challenging to set healthy boundaries in my romantic relationships. I believe this is because I grew up without a father figure, which resulted in me developing an anxious attachment style. I was always afraid of being left alone, leading me to go to great lengths to maintain my relationships. Unfortunately, this often meant I would ignore my instincts and violate my boundaries.

The term "no" used to be foreign to me since I perceived it as a weakness and a way of letting others down. I used to agree to everything, even if I couldn't follow through, leaving me guilty. In Matthew 5:37, Jesus says, "Just say a simple, 'Yes, I will,' or 'No, I won't.' Anything beyond this is from the evil one.." I didn't realize that saying yes to everything out of fear and not keeping my oath made me seem unreliable and went against God's Word.

After much-needed time with God, I realized that making false commitments to people and disregarding godly boundaries in relationships was not aligned with my values. Hence, I decided to be more assertive and confident in upholding my beliefs and establishing healthy relationships.

Boundaries are the limits we set to protect our physical, emotional, and spiritual well-being. They are essential for maintaining healthy relationships with others and ourselves. Developing boundaries is crucial to living a godly life, as they help us honor God, ourselves, and others.

The Role of the Holy Spirit in Guiding Boundaries

Setting and maintaining boundaries can be a difficult task for many of us. There could be several reasons why you may be struggling with this. Maybe you fear confrontation or don't want to disappoint others. Perhaps you fear being perceived as selfish or don't know how to say "no" without feeling guilty. Whatever the reason, it's essential to understand that setting boundaries is crucial for your emotional and mental well-being.

In living a Christian life, godly boundaries are those that align with biblical principles and reflect God's will. They are not about building walls to keep people out but rather about creating a safe space where love, respect, and integrity can thrive. These boundaries help us navigate our interactions and relationships in a way that honors God and promotes our spiritual growth.

The Holy Spirit plays a crucial role in helping us establish and maintain godly boundaries. As our counselor and guide, the Holy Spirit convicts us of sin, leads us into truth, and empowers us to live according to God's will (John 16:13). Through prayer and discernment, we can seek the Holy Spirit's guidance in identifying areas where we need to set boundaries and receive the strength to uphold them.

Biblical Principles of Boundaries

The Bible teaches us that boundaries are part of God's design for our lives. In Genesis, God sets the first boundary by placing Adam and Eve in the Garden of Eden and instructing them not to eat from the tree of the knowledge of good and evil (Genesis 2:16–17). This command establishes a clear boundary intended to protect them and guide their behavior.

Jesus Himself set boundaries during His ministry. He often withdrew from the crowds to pray and rest (Luke 5:16), demonstrating the importance of self-care and spiritual rejuvenation. He also set boundaries in His relationships, choosing His close disciples carefully and setting limits on His interactions with others.

Boundaries have a strong theological foundation rooted in the teachings of the Bible. Scripture provides numerous examples and principles that highlight the importance of boundaries in living a life that honors God.

Examples of Boundaries in the Bible

1. **Physical Boundaries:** The Old Testament laws include numerous physical boundaries, such as dietary restrictions and purity laws, which were meant to distinguish the Israelites from other nations and promote holiness (Leviticus 11).

Physical boundaries refer to our bodies and personal space, involving respecting our own and others' physical limits, including personal space and physical touch. Setting physical boundaries helps protect our bodies from harm and ensures that our personal space is respected.

2. **Emotional Boundaries and Relational Boundaries:**
    Proverbs offers wisdom on emotional boundaries and re-
    lational boundaries, advising us to guard our hearts (Prov-
    erbs 4:23) and avoid entangling ourselves in unnecessary
    conflicts (Proverbs 26:17).

Emotional boundaries involve separating our feelings
from those of others. They help us to protect our emotional
well-being by managing our responses and not taking on the
emotions or problems of others. Emotional boundaries enable
us to maintain our own emotional health and avoid becoming
overwhelmed by others' issues.

Relational boundaries involve managing our interactions and
relationships with others. These boundaries help us to establish healthy, respectful, and mutually beneficial relationships.
Relational boundaries can include setting limits on the time
and energy we invest in certain relationships and ensuring that
our interactions align with our values and beliefs.

3. **Spiritual Boundaries:** Paul's letters to the early churches
    often emphasize the importance of spiritual boundaries.
    For example, he advises the Corinthians to avoid associ-
    ations with immoral individuals to protect their spiritual
    health (1 Corinthians 5:9–13).

Spiritual boundaries are about maintaining our relationship
with God and protecting our spiritual health. These boundaries help us to prioritize our time with God, avoid spiritual
distractions, and engage in practices that nurture our faith.

Understanding and setting physical, emotional, spiritual, and
relational boundaries helps us create a balanced and healthy
life that honors God and supports our overall well-being. Each
type of boundary plays a crucial role in protecting different

aspects of our lives and helping us navigate our interactions and relationships effectively.

Identifying the Need for Boundaries

Recognizing the need for boundaries is the first step in developing and maintaining them. Several signs can indicate that we lack boundaries or that our existing boundaries need adjustment.

Signs of Lacking Boundaries

1. You don't have a close enough relationship with God.

As a lukewarm Christian, I realized my life lacked structure and purpose. I soon discovered that my lackluster relationship with God was the root cause of my struggles. I rarely prayed or took the time to read the Bible. Moreover, I was unfamiliar with the concept of godly boundaries and how to establish them.

Establishing and maintaining godly boundaries is a crucial aspect of building a healthy and fulfilling life. It involves recognizing and respecting our own values, needs, and limitations, as well as those of others. However, this is not always an easy task, as we live in a world that often encourages us to compromise our principles and go against our better judgment.

That is why it is vital to develop a deeper relationship with God through prayer and reading His Word. By doing so, we can gain wisdom, guidance, and strength to resist temptation, overcome challenges, and make wise decisions that honor God and benefit ourselves and others. Through prayer, we can seek God's will and ask for His help and protection in all areas of our lives.

By reading His Word, we can learn more about His character, promises, and plans for our lives and be inspired to live according to His truth and grace. Ultimately, by prioritizing our relationship with God, we can establish godly boundaries that reflect His love and wisdom and experience the abundant life He promised to those who seek Him first.

2. You are a people-pleaser.

When you are always looking to please those around you, you may delegate a lot of time and energy to meeting their expectations. While there's nothing wrong with being kind and considerate, it's important to remember that putting too much emphasis on the opinions of others can be harmful in the long run. Sometimes, when we care too much about what other people think, we end up idolizing them and losing sight of our values, dreams, and desires. In Galatians 1:10, the apostle Paul reminds us to focus on pleasing God rather than constantly seeking the approval of others. By staying faithful to God, we can live a more meaningful and fulfilling life, regardless of what others think or say.

3. You fear being abandoned or losing something important to you.

Growing up without the presence of my father had a profound impact on me. It led me to develop a deep-seated fear of abandonment and loss, which caused me to constantly pursue perfection in every aspect of my life. I felt that any mistake or failure on my part would result in losing everything I had worked so hard for. This fear was a constant struggle as I tried to let go of it and trust that what was meant for me would eventually come my way.

Throughout my journey, I have realized that conquering my fears and overcoming my struggles required me to prioritize pleasing and obeying God above all else. I have learned that God is the ultimate provider, and if I trust Him, He will take care of everything. This realization has brought me peace and allowed me to move forward with a renewed sense of purpose.

Seeking Wisdom from Scripture and Mentors

The Bible provides wisdom on boundaries, and seeking counsel from scripture can help us understand God's design for healthy boundaries. Additionally, mentors or trusted friends can offer valuable insights and advice on setting and maintaining boundaries. Their experience and perspective can help us identify areas where we need to improve our boundaries and provide support in the process.

By recognizing the signs of lacking boundaries, engaging in personal reflection and prayer, and seeking wisdom from scripture and mentors, we can identify the areas in our lives that need boundaries. This awareness is the foundation for developing godly boundaries that will protect our well-being and honor God.

Steps to Develop Godly Boundaries

Developing godly boundaries involves a series of intentional steps. These steps help us to create boundaries that protect our well-being and honor God.

Self-Awareness and Self-Assessment

The first step in developing boundaries is self-awareness. We need to understand our needs, values, and limits. Self-assessment involves reflecting on our experiences and identifying areas where we struggle with boundaries. This can be done through prayer, journaling, and seeking feedback from trusted friends or mentors.

Setting Clear and Realistic Boundaries

Once we have a clear understanding of our needs and limits, we can begin to set boundaries. These boundaries should be specific, clear, and realistic. It's important to define what we are comfortable with and what we are not. For example, setting a boundary might involve limiting the amount of time we spend on certain activities or with certain people.

Communicating Boundaries Effectively

Effective communication is crucial in setting boundaries. Clearly and respectfully articulating our boundaries with others helps ensure they understand our needs and limits. When communicating boundaries, it is important to:

1. Be Direct: State your boundaries clearly without ambiguity.

2. Use "I" Statements: Frame your boundaries in a way that focuses on your needs and feelings. For example, "I need some time alone to recharge" rather than "You're always invading my space."

3. Be Firm but Kind: Maintain a firm stance on your boundaries while being kind and respectful to others.

4. Stay Calm: Communicate your boundaries in a calm and composed manner to avoid escalating tensions.

Enforcing and Maintaining Boundaries

Setting boundaries is only the beginning; enforcing and maintaining them is an ongoing process. Here are some strategies for maintaining boundaries:

1. Consistent Reinforcement: Regularly reinforce your boundaries to ensure they are respected. This might involve gently reminding others of your limits.

2. Self-Care: Prioritize self-care to maintain your boundaries. This includes taking time for yourself and engaging in activities that rejuvenate you.

3. Accountability Partners: Enlist the support of trusted friends or mentors who can help hold you accountable to your boundaries.

4. Adjust When Necessary: Be open to adjusting your boundaries as needed. Life circumstances change, and your boundaries may need to evolve accordingly.

Handling Resistance and Pushback

It's common to encounter resistance or pushback when setting boundaries, especially from those who are used to your old patterns. Here are some tips for handling resistance:

1. Stay Firm: Reiterate your boundaries firmly, even if others push back.

2. Explain the Importance: Help others understand why your boundaries are important for your well-being.

3. Seek Support: If you encounter significant resistance, seek support from friends, mentors, or a counselor.

4. Pray for Guidance: Pray for wisdom and strength to maintain your boundaries in the face of resistance.

Challenges in Maintaining Boundaries

Maintaining boundaries can be challenging for various reasons. Here are some common obstacles and strategies to overcome them:

Common Obstacles

1. Guilt: Feeling guilty for setting boundaries, especially if it disappoints others.

2. Fear of Rejection: Worrying that setting boundaries will lead to rejection or conflict.

3. People-Pleasing Tendencies: Struggling to say no due to a desire to please others.

4. Cultural or Family Expectations: Facing pressure from cultural or familial norms that discourage boundary-setting.

Dealing with Guilt and Fear

1. Understand the Necessity: Recognize that boundaries are essential for your well-being and that it's okay to prioritize your needs.

2. Reframe Your Thinking: Shift your perspective to see boundaries as a way to foster healthier relationships rather than as a rejection of others.

3. Practice Self-Compassion: Be kind to yourself and acknowledge that it's okay to have needs and limits.

Balancing Grace and Firmness

1. Show Compassion: While maintaining your boundaries, show compassion and understanding towards others.

2. Offer Alternatives: When possible, offer alternative solutions that respect your boundaries while addressing the other person's needs.

3. Pray for Wisdom: Seek God's guidance to strike the right balance between grace and firmness in maintaining your boundaries.

By acknowledging the challenges and implementing these strategies, we can effectively maintain our boundaries and experience the benefits they bring.

The Benefits of Godly Boundaries

Setting and maintaining godly boundaries offers numerous benefits for our personal growth, spiritual health, and relationships.

Personal Growth and Spiritual Health

1. Increased Self-Awareness: Setting boundaries helps us understand our needs and limits better.

2. Greater Peace and Clarity: Boundaries reduce stress and confusion by providing clear guidelines for our behavior and interactions.

3. Enhanced Spiritual Health: By prioritizing time with God and protecting our spiritual practices, we grow closer to Him.

Improved Relationships

1. Healthier Interactions: Boundaries foster respect and mutual understanding in our relationships.

2. Reduced Conflict: Clear boundaries help to prevent misunderstandings and conflicts.

3. Stronger Connections: Boundaries allow us to engage in relationships more authentically and meaningfully.

Greater Peace and Clarity

1. Focus on Priorities: Boundaries enable us to focus on what truly matters, aligning our actions with our values and goals.

2. Balanced Life: By protecting our time and energy, boundaries help us to achieve a more balanced and fulfilling life.

Overall, godly boundaries empower us to live more intentional, peaceful, and spiritually enriched lives. They enhance our well-being and relationships, allowing us to honor God and fulfill our purpose more effectively.

Developing godly boundaries is essential for living a life that honors God.. Boundaries protect our physical, emotional, spiritual, and relational health, enabling us to navigate our interactions and relationships in a way that aligns with biblical principles.

By understanding the theological foundation of boundaries, recognizing the signs of lacking boundaries, and implementing practical steps to set and maintain them, we can create a balanced and healthy life. Effective communication, consistent reinforcement, and handling resistance with grace and firmness are crucial to maintaining our boundaries.

Despite the challenges, the benefits of setting godly boundaries are immense. They contribute to our personal growth, enhance our spiritual health, and improve our relationships. By prioritizing our needs and aligning our actions with our values, we can experience greater peace, clarity, and fulfillment.

In my personal experience, I have found that letting go of things that no longer serve me has opened up new opportunities and blessings in my life. It's not always easy to let go, but I have learned to trust in God's plan for me and to have faith that He will guide me in the right direction. By prioritizing my relationship with God above all else, I have found a sense of purpose and fulfillment in my life that I never thought was possible.

As we strive to develop and maintain godly boundaries, let us seek God's guidance and rely on the Holy Spirit to lead us. Through prayer, reflection, and the support of trusted mentors, we can create boundaries that honor God and enrich our lives.

I encourage you to take the time to assess your current boundaries, identify areas for improvement, and implement the steps outlined. By doing so, you will be better equipped to live a life that honors God, respects your well-being, and fosters healthy, meaningful relationships.

1. Self-Awareness and Boundaries:

What are some specific instances in your past relationships where your boundaries were violated? How did these experiences affect you emotionally, spiritually, and physically?

2. Attachment and Fear:

How have your fears of abandonment and being left alone influenced your behavior in relationships? How can you begin to address these fears in a healthy way?

3. The Role of "No":

How do you feel when you have to say "no" to someone? What steps can you take to become more comfortable with asserting your boundaries and saying "no" when necessary?

4. Spiritual Guidance and Boundaries:

In what ways can you seek the Holy Spirit's guidance to help you establish and maintain godly boundaries? How can incorporating prayer and scripture reading into your daily routine support this process?

5. Personal Growth and Accountability:

What are some practical steps you can take to reinforce your boundaries consistently? How can you enlist the support of trusted friends, mentors, or accountability partners to help you stay on track?

CHAPTER 11

THE POWER OF FORGIVENESS: HEALING THROUGH GRACE

Encountering consistent trauma and pain over a prolonged period can be an incredibly challenging and distressing experience. It can lead to bitterness, anger, and resentment towards yourself and others. These negative emotions can take over your life, making it difficult to find peace and happiness. At times, the idea of forgiveness can seem almost impossible. You may feel that forgiving someone means you are letting them off the hook for the pain they caused you or that you are somehow weak for not holding onto your anger and resentment.

Understanding Forgiveness

Forgiveness can be defined as the act of pardoning an offender and letting go of resentment or vengeance. It is a conscious decision to release feelings of anger or retribution against someone who has wronged you.

Forgiveness is a process necessary for leading a healthy and happy life. It involves releasing negative emotions and resentment towards someone who has caused you pain and finding a way to move forward without allowing that pain to control your life. It requires a deep sense of compassion, empathy, and understanding towards yourself and others.

Biblical Basis for Forgiveness

Forgiveness is a central theme in the Bible, woven throughout its pages from Genesis to Revelation. It is a moral ideal and a divine mandate reflecting God's heart. Understanding and practicing biblical forgiveness opens our hearts to healing, peace, and closer relationships with God and others.

The Bible provides numerous teachings on the importance of forgiveness. In Matthew 6:14–15, Jesus emphasizes the necessity of forgiving others: "If you forgive those who sin against you, your heavenly Father will forgive you. But if you refuse to forgive others, your Father will not forgive your sins.". Similarly, Ephesians 4:32 instructs believers to "Instead be kind to each other, tenderhearted, forgiving one another, just as God through Christ has forgiven you."

The Role of the Heart in Forgiveness

True forgiveness starts from the heart. It is not merely an external act but an internal transformation that reflects God's love.

The Parable of the Unforgiving Servant

In Matthew 18:21–35, Jesus shares the parable of the unforgiving servant to illustrate the importance of forgiving from the heart. The servant who was forgiven for a massive debt by his master refused to forgive a fellow servant for a much smaller debt, showing a hardened heart that ultimately led to his downfall.

Love is also an essential factor in forgiveness. In John 13:34, Jesus emphasizes the significance of unconditional love for one another. He proclaims, "So now I am giving you a new commandment: Love each other. Just as I have loved you, you should love each other." These words serve as a reminder of how crucial it is to love one another. However, it is impossible to love unconditionally while holding unforgiveness in your heart.

Forgiveness enables us to let go of the pain and negative emotions that hinder us, while love allows us to comprehend that the person who hurt us may not have acted out of their own volition. By choosing to operate in love, we will be more inclined to pray for the person's salvation, as it is only through love and forgiveness that we can genuinely heal and move forward. This commandment is not just a suggestion but a vital aspect of our spiritual journey. By following this commandment, we can better connect with God.

The story of Joseph, found in Genesis 37–50, is a powerful example of the importance of forgiveness. Despite being sold into slavery by his brothers, Joseph eventually rose to a position of power and was able to save his family from famine. However, his entire purpose would have been derailed if he had not forgiven his brothers for their betrayal.

The act of forgiveness is a powerful and transformative journey that can have a tremendous impact on our lives. Forgiveness is not always easy, especially when we have been deeply hurt by someone else's actions. Joseph faced a difficult decision when choosing between punishing or forgiving his brothers. Despite the pain and betrayal he experienced, he decided to forgive them and move on with his life. This act of forgiveness was a testament to his strength, courage, and humility.

Steps to Forgive Others

Acknowledge the Hurt

The first step in forgiveness is acknowledging the pain and hurt caused by the offense. Denying or minimizing the hurt can prevent true forgiveness.

Reflect on Jesus' Teachings

Reflecting on scriptures like Luke 6:37 ("Do not judge others, and you will not be judged. Do not condemn others, or it will all come back against you. Forgive others, and you will be forgiven.") and Mark 11:25 ("But when you are praying, first forgive anyone you are holding a grudge against, so that your Father in heaven will forgive your sins, too.") can provide the spiritual motivation to forgive.

Pray for Strength and Guidance

Prayer is essential in the process of forgiveness. Ask God for the strength and wisdom to forgive, as well as for healing from the hurt.

Release the Offender

Letting go of resentment and the desire for revenge is a crucial step. This involves consciously releasing the offender from any debt they owe you emotionally or spiritually.

Practical Tips for Forgiving Others

- Write a letter to the offender (even if you don't send it) expressing your feelings and decision to forgive.
- Talk to a trusted friend or counselor about your feelings.

- Engage in acts of kindness towards the offender if possible.

- Remember and reflect on your own need for forgiveness.

Forgiveness vs. Reconciliation

Forgiveness and reconciliation are different processes. Forgiveness is a personal journey for the offended party, allowing them to let go of anger and resentment. On the other hand, reconciliation involves both parties actively participating and being willing to mend their relationship and rebuild trust. While forgiveness can be an important step in the reconciliation process, it does not guarantee reconciliation will occur.

Forgiving someone does not mean you have to reconcile with them. Sometimes, forgiving and moving on are all God calls you to do.

Forgiving Yourself

Understanding Self-Forgiveness in a Biblical Context

Forgiveness is not just about pardoning others but also about pardoning ourselves. Accepting our blunders and freeing ourselves from the guilt and shame that accompany them can be a strenuous and prolonged process. Nevertheless, it is a vital aspect of personal growth and recovery.

It is often more difficult to forgive ourselves than to forgive others. We usually hold ourselves to very high standards and find it challenging to let go of our past mistakes. Sometimes, we may feel undeserving of forgiveness, making the process even more arduous. However, it is essential to comprehend that making mistakes is a natural part of being human, and we can learn from them to become better individuals.

When we forgive ourselves, we give ourselves the priceless gift of freedom. Through forgiveness, we let go of the weighty burden of guilt and shame and wholeheartedly embrace the present moment. It's worth noting that forgiveness is not an instant or one-time occurrence but rather a gradual process that calls for patience, compassion, and understanding.

I found forgiving myself for my past mistakes extremely difficult for a long time. I had engaged in behaviors that I was not proud of, and I felt that no godly man would ever consider being with me. This belief was so ingrained in me that even after I gave my life to Jesus, I continued to live in shame and regret for a year.

I carried a sense of shame deep within me, which led me to make poor choices in my relationships. I believed that only toxic men would be interested in me, and as a result, I found myself trapped in a cycle of attracting and choosing partners who were not good for me. This pattern only reinforced my negative beliefs about myself, and it was a challenging cycle to break.

However, as I began to delve deeper into the Word of God, I came across 2 Corinthians 5:17, where the Apostle Paul speaks about the transformative power of Christ in a believer's life. He notes that when someone becomes a follower of Christ, they are essentially reborn as a new creation. This means that their old way of living and thinking, along with their sins and shortcomings, are washed away and replaced with a new nature centered on living for God. This profound transformation marks a new beginning for the believers as they strive to live a life pleasing to God and in line with His will.

During my journey toward personal growth and self-discovery, I underwent a transformative experience that made me realize that my old patterns and behaviors no longer defined me.

They were part of my past; I was now a new creation, ready to embrace a better version of myself. However, this transformation was not easy, and I faced several challenges. In times of doubt and uncertainty, I found solace in the teachings of the Bible, particularly in a verse that had a profound impact on my perspective: Psalm 86:5

This scripture says, "O Lord, you are so good, so ready to forgive, so full of unfailing love for all who ask for your help." These words reminded me that God is forgiving and loving, and the enemy constantly reminded me of my past. It was a powerful realization that helped me understand that God convicts through love, which is temporary, but the enemy condemns.

With this newfound understanding, I could break free from the chains of my past and move forward with confidence and hope. I learned to let go of my past mistakes and embrace the person I was becoming.

Self-forgiveness is about accepting God's forgiveness and extending that grace to yourself. It is not about ignoring or minimizing your sins, but recognizing that through Christ, you are forgiven.

Psalm 103:12 reassures us: "He has removed our sins as far from us as the east is from the west." Similarly, 1 John 3:20 states, "Even if we feel guilty, God is greater than our feelings, and he knows everything."

Practical Steps to Forgive Yourself

- Acknowledge your mistakes and confess them to God.
- Accept God's forgiveness and His promise of cleansing.
- Remind yourself of your identity in Christ—you are a new creation.

- Practice self-compassion and avoid self-condemnation.

God has a beautiful purpose for each of our lives, and it is only by becoming a child of God and giving our lives to Jesus that we can receive it. However, being saved is just the beginning of a lifelong process called sanctification, where God prunes us to become more like Him. In this process, we learn to forgive ourselves and others, which is crucial for our spiritual growth.

I experienced the power of forgiveness when I was scammed out of $2800. At first, I was devastated and felt like I had been taken advantage of. However, I knew that I could not allow that pain to consume me. Instead, I turned to prayer and began praying for the person who had scammed me daily. It was not easy, but it helped me to see him as someone who needed Jesus rather than someone to hate.

Seeking Forgiveness

Recognizing the Need for Forgiveness

It's crucial to recognize and acknowledge when you have hurt someone. This is a vital part of emotional intelligence and personal growth. Understanding the impact of your actions on others and taking responsibility for your mistakes is the first step toward healing and rebuilding trust in relationships. Seeking forgiveness shows empathy and a genuine desire to make amends, which can lead to inner peace and stronger connections with others.

1 John 1:9 says, "But if we confess our sins to him, he is faithful and just to forgive us our sins and to cleanse us from all wickedness." Genuine confession and repentance are foundational in the process of seeking forgiveness.

Making Amends and Restitution

When you realize that you have made a mistake or hurt someone, taking responsibility for your actions is important. Making amends involves acknowledging the harm you've caused, sincerely apologizing, and taking concrete steps to repair the damage. You demonstrate your genuine remorse and commitment to making things right by offering restitution. This can help rebuild trust and show dedication to positive change and personal growth.

Accepting Forgiveness

Accepting forgiveness from others can be difficult, but it is essential for healing and moving forward. Embrace the grace extended to you and allow it to foster personal growth and renewed relationships.

Living a Forgiving Life

Daily Practices for Maintaining a Forgiving Heart

- Engage in daily prayer and reflection.

- Read and meditate on scriptures about forgiveness.

- Surround yourself with a supportive community that encourages forgiveness.

Benefits of a Forgiving Lifestyle

Living a life filled with forgiveness has many positive effects. When we choose to forgive, we experience spiritual growth as we let go of negative emotions and open our hearts to compassion and understanding. Emotionally, forgiveness can lead to healing and release from anger and resentment. This freedom allows us to cultivate healthier and more fulfilling relationships with others. Forgiveness enables us to experience a more profound sense of peace and contentment.

Forgiveness is a journey that requires divine strength and grace. Following the steps outlined and relying on God's guidance, we can cultivate a forgiving heart, experience healing, and build stronger, more loving relationships.

You are a valuable creation of God, and He wants you to live a life filled with love, joy, and purpose. So, prioritize forgiveness and take concrete actions to heal your heart and soul.

Let us strive to live a life marked by forgiveness, reflecting the love and grace of our Heavenly Father.

1. Acknowledge the Hurt:

Reflect on a specific instance where someone hurt you deeply. How did this experience impact you emotionally, spiritually, and mentally? Write about the emotions you felt and how this incident has shaped your current outlook on forgiveness.

2. Reflect on Jesus' Teachings:

Think about a time when you struggled to forgive someone. How can the teachings of Jesus, such as those in Matthew 6:14-15 and Ephesians 4:32, guide you in this process? How do these scriptures resonate with your personal experiences and challenges?

3. The Role of the Heart in Forgiveness:

Describe a situation where you found it difficult to forgive from the heart. What steps did you take (or can you take) to transform your heart and let go of resentment? How does understanding forgiveness as an internal transformation change your perspective?

4. Forgiving Yourself:

Recall a time when you found it hard to forgive yourself for a mistake or past behavior. What scriptures or spiritual insights helped you move toward self-forgiveness? How has forgiving yourself impacted your relationship with God and others?

5. Living a Forgiving Life:

Identify daily practices you can incorporate to maintain a forgiving heart. How can prayer, reflection, and scripture reading help you cultivate forgiveness? What benefits have you experienced or hope to experience from leading a life marked by forgiveness?

CLOSING REMARKS: EMBRACING GOD'S PLAN AND PURPOSE FOR YOUR LIFE

For years, I was disobedient to God. I refused to be single, driven by a desperation to have a relationship. My fear of being alone clouded my judgment and led me down paths unaligned with God's will for my life. I sought validation and love from men, believing a relationship would complete me. This relentless pursuit brought pain, heartache, and a sense of emptiness that no relationship could fill.

It wasn't until I finally surrendered everything to God and embraced singleness that my life changed. In this season of being single, I discovered a clarity of purpose that had eluded me for years. This book is a testament to that journey of healing, self-discovery, and, most importantly, a deepening relationship with God. I want every woman reading this to understand that you are a child of God and immensely valuable. God knows exactly what you need and will never steer you in the wrong direction.

Embracing Singleness: A Season of Growth

When I finally gave everything to God and accepted singleness, I began a profound growth season. For the first time, I began to focus on my relationship with God rather than on finding a relationship with a man. This shift in focus transformed my life in ways I could never have imagined.

Singleness is often viewed as a negative state—a period of waiting or a time of lack. But I learned that singleness is a gift, a precious opportunity to grow closer to God and to understand His unique purpose for my life. During this time, I learned to see myself through God's eyes, not through the lens of my past mistakes or the world's expectations.

I want you to know that being single does not mean you are incomplete. You are whole and complete in Christ. This season of singleness is a time to discover who you are in Him, develop your gifts and talents, and prepare for His plans for your future. It is a time to build a strong foundation in your faith that will sustain you through all of life's challenges.

Discovering Your Purpose

One of the most significant transformations during my season of singleness was discovering my purpose. I had been looking for my identity and worth in relationships for so long. But when I turned my focus to God, He began to reveal the unique purpose He had for my life.

Jeremiah 29:11 says, "For I know the plans I have for you," says the Lord. "They are plans for good and not for disaster, to give you a future and a hope." This promise is true for each one of us. God has a specific plan for your life and desires to see you fulfill it.

As I spent more time in prayer and studying the Bible, God began to place a vision in my heart. He showed me that my experiences, pain, and journey were not in vain. He had a purpose for them. He wanted me to use my story to help other women struggling with the same issues I had faced. This book is a result of that vision.

Your purpose may look different from mine, but know that it is equally significant. God has placed unique gifts, talents, and passions within you. He wants to use them to make a difference in the world. Take this time to seek Him, to ask Him to reveal His plans for you, and to trust that He will guide you every step of the way.

Valuing Yourself as a Child of God

Understanding your value as a child of God is crucial. For years, I allowed the opinions of others and my desire for a relationship to define my worth. However, my journey taught me that external factors do not determine my value. It is determined by the One who created me.

As a reminder, Psalm 139:14 says, "I praise you because I am fearfully and wonderfully made; your works are wonderful; I know that full well." You are fearfully and wonderfully made by a loving Creator who sees you as precious.

Embracing this truth changed everything for me. It gave me the confidence to set boundaries, walk away from unhealthy relationships, and pursue the life God had for me. I want you to know that you are valuable. You are loved. You are worthy of respect and kindness. Do not settle for anything less than what God has for you.

Trusting God's Plan

One of the most challenging aspects of my journey was learning to trust God's plan. It required me to let go of my desires and to trust that God knew what was best for me. This was not easy, especially when I didn't understand why things were happening as they were.

But over time, I began to see that God's plans are always better than mine. He sees the bigger picture. He knows what we need even before we do. Proverbs 3:5–6 says, "Trust in the Lord with all your heart; do not depend on your own understanding. Seek his will in all you do, and he will show you which path to take."

Trusting God means surrendering your fears, doubts, and need for control. It means believing He is good, even when life doesn't make sense. It means knowing that He is faithful and will never leave or forsake you.

As I trusted God more, I began to experience His peace and provision in ways I never had before. He opened doors I never could have imagined and miraculously provided for me. I learned that when you trust God, you will never be disappointed.

Encouraging Others

One of the greatest joys of my journey has been the opportunity to encourage and inspire others. Sharing my story, my struggles, and my victories has not only brought healing to my own heart but has also helped others find hope and healing in their own lives.

I want to encourage you to share your story. Your experiences, pain, and triumphs can be a source of encouragement and inspiration to others. You never know how your story might impact someone else's life.

Hebrews 10:24–25 says, "Let us think of ways to motivate one another to acts of love and good works. And let us not neglect our meeting together, as some people do, but encourage one another, especially now that the day of His return is drawing near."

We are called to encourage one another, to lift each other, and to walk alongside each other in this journey of faith. Your story matters. Your voice matters. Don't be afraid to share it.

Embracing God's Healing

Healing is a journey, and it often takes time. There were moments in my journey when I felt like I would never heal from the pain of my past. But God is faithful, and He is a healer. Psalm 147:3 says, "He heals the brokenhearted and bandages their wounds."

God's healing is not just physical but emotional, mental, and spiritual. He wants to heal every part of you. He wants to restore what has been broken and make your life whole.

As you walk this journey of healing, be patient with yourself. Allow yourself to feel the pain and grieve the losses. But also allow yourself to hope, dream, and believe that God has a beautiful future for you.

Surround yourself with a supportive community of believers who can walk alongside you, pray for you, and encourage you. Seek professional help if needed. Healing is a process, but with God, all things are possible.

Living with Purpose

As I embraced God's plan for my life and allowed Him to heal my heart, I began living with a purpose I had never known before. I realized that my life had meaning and that God had a specific mission for me.

Living with purpose means living intentionally. It means seeking God's will in every area of your life and aligning your actions with His plans. It means using your gifts and talents to serve others and to bring glory to God.

Ephesians 2:10 says, "For we are God's masterpiece. He has created us anew in Christ Jesus, so we can do the good things he planned for us long ago." You have a purpose. God has prepared good works for you to do, and He wants to use you to make a difference in the world.

Final Encouragement

As I bring this book to a close, my heart is filled with gratitude for the journey God has brought me on. It has been a healing journey, a transformation, and a discovery of my true identity in Christ. I am not the same person I was, and I am so thankful for God's work in my life.

I want to leave you with a few final words of encouragement:

1. Seek God First: Matthew 6:33 says, "Seek the Kingdom of God above all else, and live righteously, and he will give you everything you need." Make your relationship with God your top priority. Everything else will fall into place when you seek Him first.

2. Trust God's Timing: Ecclesiastes 3:11 says, "He has made everything beautiful for its own time." Trust that God's timing is perfect. He knows what is best for you and will bring it to pass in His perfect timing.

3. Embrace Your Worth: Know that you are valuable and loved by God. You are His precious child, and He has a beautiful plan for your life. Don't settle for anything less than what God has for you.

4. Live with Purpose: Discover God's unique purpose for your life and live it out with passion and intention. Use your gifts and talents to serve others and to bring glory to God.

5. Stay in Community: Surround yourself with a supportive community of believers who can walk alongside you, pray for you, and encourage you in your faith journey. We are not meant to walk this journey alone. The body of Christ is a powerful support system designed to uplift, edify, and challenge us to grow. Hebrews 10:24–25 reminds us of the importance of fellowship: "Let us think of ways to motivate one another to acts of love and good works. And let us not neglect our meeting together, as some people do, but encourage one another, especially now that the day of his return is drawing near."

A Life Transformed

Reflecting on my journey, I am filled with awe at how God has transformed my life. From a place of desperation and disobedience, He has brought me into a season of purpose and fulfillment. I now understand that true contentment comes from a deep relationship with God, not from the approval or love of others.

God's faithfulness has been evident in every step of my journey. He has taken my brokenness and made something beautiful out of it. He has turned my pain into a platform for ministry, allowing me to share His love and grace with others.

CONCLUSION

Thank you for allowing me to share my journey with you. It has been an honor to walk this path of healing and discovery alongside you. My prayer is that you have been encouraged, inspired, and equipped to embrace your journey with God.

Remember that you are a child of God, fearfully and wonderfully made. He has a beautiful plan for your life and desires to see you walk in the fullness of His love and purpose. Trust in Him, seek Him with all your heart, and watch as He transforms your life in ways you could never have imagined.

May God bless you abundantly as you continue to seek His will and walk in His ways. May you experience His peace, joy, and love in every area of your life. May you always remember that, with God, all things are possible.

In His love and grace,

Nikki Lewis

www.ingramcontent.com/pod-product-compliance
Lightning Source LLC
Chambersburg PA
CBHW050522160726
48003CB00001B/419